Exam Success
Plumbing and Heating 6189-11 and 6189-21

© 2011 The City and Guilds of London Institute

City & Guilds is a trademark of the City and Guilds of London Institute

ISBN: 9780851931944

Every effort has been made to ensure that the information contained in this publication is true and correct at the time of going to press. However, examination products and services are subject to continuous development and improvement and the right is reserved to change products and services from time to time. While the author, publishers and contributors believe that the information and guidance given in this work is correct, all parties must rely upon their own skill and judgement when making use of it. Neither the author, the publishers nor any contributor assume any liability to anyone for any loss or damage caused by any error or omission in the work, whether such error or omission is the result of negligence or any other cause. Where reference is made to legislation it is not to be considered as legal advice. Any and all such liability is disclaimed.

Cover and book design by CDT Design Ltd
Typeset in Congress Sans and Gotham by Select Typesetters Limited
Printed in the UK by Sterling

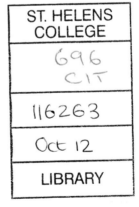

Exam Success
Plumbing and Heating 6189-11 and 6189-21

City & Guilds is the UK's leading provider of vocational qualifications, offering over 500 awards across a wide range of industries, and progressing from entry level to the highest levels of professional achievement. With over 8500 centres in 100 countries, City & Guilds is recognised by employers worldwide for providing qualifications that offer proof of the skills they need to get the job done.

Copies may be obtained from:
Publishing (WS3)
City & Guilds
1 Giltspur Street
London EC1A 9DD
For publications enquiries:
T +44 (0)844 543 0033
F +44 (0)20 7294 2400
Email learningsupport@cityandguilds.com

Contents

Introduction

How to use this book

This book has been written as a study aid for the
– City & Guilds NVQ Level 2 Diploma in Plumbing & Heating (6189-11)
– City & Guilds NVQ Level 2 Diploma in Domestic Heating (6189-21).

Both diplomas are entry-level qualifications into either the plumbing and heating industry or the specialist domestic heating industry. The main difference between the two qualifications is that the specialist domestic heating route does not incorporate skills and knowledge in the installation of sanitation equipment eg bathroom installation, sanitation or rainwater pipework installation.

The unit structure for the City & Guilds NVQ Level 2 Diploma in Plumbing & Heating (6189-11) route is shown below.

City & Guilds number	Unit title
001	Understand and carry out **safe working practices** in building services engineering
002	Understand how to **communicate** with others within building services engineering
003	Understand how to apply **environmental protection measures** within building services engineering
004	Understand how to apply **scientific principles** within mechanical engineering services
005	Understand and carry out **site preparation, and pipework fabrication techniques** for domestic plumbing and heating systems
006	Understand and apply **domestic cold water system** installation and maintenance techniques
007	Understand and apply **domestic hot water system** installation and maintenance techniques
008	Understand and apply **domestic central heating system** installation and maintenance techniques
009	Understand and apply **domestic rainwater system** installation and maintenance techniques
010	Understand and apply **domestic above-ground drainage system** installation and maintenance techniques
019	Apply **safe working practices** in the building services engineering working environment
020	**Install and maintain** domestic plumbing and heating systems

Notes

The unit structure for the City & Guilds NVQ Level 2 Diploma in Domestic Heating (6189-21) route is shown below.

City & Guilds number	Unit title
001	Understand and carry out **safe working practices** in building services engineering
002	Understand how to **communicate** with others within building services engineering
003	Understand how to apply **environmental protection measures** within building services engineering
004	Understand how to apply **scientific principles** within mechanical engineering services
005	Understand and carry out **site preparation, and pipework fabrication techniques** for domestic plumbing and heating systems
006	Understand and apply **domestic cold water system** installation and maintenance techniques
007	Understand and apply **domestic hot water system** installation and maintenance techniques
008	Understand and apply **domestic central heating system** installation and maintenance techniques
019	Apply **safe working practices** in the building services engineering working environment
022	**Install and maintain domestic heating** systems

Both diplomas contain a number of mandatory units, which must be completed to achieve the full qualification. Each diploma contains a number of units (colour coded in the charts) that are either:

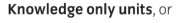 **Knowledge only units**, or

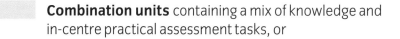 **Combination units** containing a mix of knowledge and in-centre practical assessment tasks, or

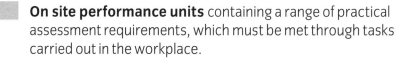 **On site performance units** containing a range of practical assessment requirements, which must be met through tasks carried out in the workplace.

The purpose of this Exam Success publication is to provide support to assist in successful completion of the knowledge elements of the qualification programmes. This book covers units 005–010 and sets out methods of studying, offers advice on exam preparation and provides details of the scope and structure of the knowledge examinations, alongside sample questions with fully worked-through answers. Used as a study guide for exam preparation and practice, it will help you to reinforce and test your existing knowledge, and will give you guidelines and advice about sitting the exams. You should try to answer the sample test questions under exam conditions (or as close as you can get) and then review all of your answers. This will help you to become familiar with the types of questions that might be asked in the exams and also give you an idea of how to pace yourself in order to complete all questions comfortably within the time limit. This book cannot guarantee a positive exam result, but it can play an important role in your overall revision programme, enabling you to focus your preparation and approach the exams with confidence.

Finding a centre
In order to take the exams, you must register at an approved City & Guilds centre. You can find your nearest centre by looking up the qualification number 6189 on www.cityandguilds.com.

At each centre, the Local Examinations Secretary will enter you for the award, collect your fees, arrange for your assessment to take place and correspond with City & Guilds on your behalf. The Local Examinations Secretary also receives all of your certificates and correspondence from City & Guilds. Most centres will require you to attend a course of learning before entering you for the examinations. The duration of this course will vary depending upon whether you have any previous plumbing and heating knowledge and skills that can contribute to the learning programme. Ask your chosen centre for further details.

Awarding and reporting
When you complete the City & Guilds 6189 Diploma online examinations, you will be given your provisional results, as well as a breakdown of your performance in the various areas of the examination. This is a useful diagnostic tool if you fail the exams, as it enables you to identify your individual strengths and weaknesses across the different topics.

Notes

Notes

A certificate is issued automatically when you have been successful in the assessment, but it will not indicate a grade or percentage pass. Your centre will receive your Notification of Candidate's Results. Any correspondence is conducted through the centre. The centre will also receive a consolidated results list detailing the performance of all candidates entered. If you have particular requirements that will affect your ability to attend and take the examination, then your centre should refer to City & Guilds' policy document 'Access to Assessment: Candidates with Particular Requirements'.

The exam

The exam

The examinations are in a multiple-choice format, with each examination containing a different number of questions based on the topic area of the unit. The exams are therefore of varying maximum duration (details shown below). The test is offered on GOLA (Global Online Assessment), a simple online service that does not require strong IT skills. GOLA uses a bank of questions set and approved by City & Guilds. Each candidate receives randomised questions, so no two candidates will sit exactly the same test.

City & Guilds number	Unit title	No. of questions	Duration (mins.)
001	Understand and carry out **safe working practices** in building services engineering	55	110
002	Understand how to **communicate** with others within building services engineering	20	40
003	Understand how to apply **environmental protection** measures within building services engineering	25	50
004	Understand how to apply **scientific principles** within mechanical engineering services	40	80
005	Understand and carry out **site preparation, and pipework fabrication techniques** for domestic plumbing and heating systems	50	100
006	Understand and apply **domestic cold water system** installation and maintenance techniques	55	110
007	Understand and apply **domestic hot water system** installation and maintenance techniques	60	120
008	Understand and apply **domestic central heating system** installation and maintenance techniques	60	120
009	Understand and apply **domestic rainwater** system installation and maintenance techniques	35	70
010	Understand and apply **domestic above-ground drainage system** installation and maintenance techniques	50	100

Units 001 to 005 are operated as closed-book examinations during which no reference materials can be used to answer the examination questions.

Units 006 to 010 are operated as open-book examinations during which a series of normative reference documents can be used to assist with answering the examination questions.

Normative reference documents are Building & Water Regulation Approved Documents (Technical Booklets in Northern Ireland) and appropriate British Standards. Relevant normative documents are listed among the items of additional reading on pages 174–175 of this publication. It's also worth noting that the normative reference sources do not contain the answers to all questions in a particular exam, particularly where the application of knowledge is required; their main purpose is to assist with providing access to information that may not be readily remembered.

Notes

Notes

Sitting a City & Guilds online examination

The test will be taken under usual exam conditions. You will not be allowed to take your mobile phone into the exam room and you cannot leave the exam room unless you are accompanied by one of the test invigilators. If you leave the exam room unaccompanied before the end of the test period, you may not be allowed to come back into the exam.

When you take a City & Guilds exam online, you can go through a tutorial to familiarise yourself with the online procedures. When you are logged on to take the exam, the first screen will give you the chance to go into a tutorial. The tutorial shows how the exam will be presented and how to get help, how to move between different screens, and how to mark questions that you want to return to later.

City& Guilds

Please work through the tutorial before you start your examination.

This will show you how to answer questions and use the menu options to help you complete the examination.

Please note that examination conditions now apply.

The time allowed for the tutorial is 10 minutes.

Click on Continue to start the tutorial or Skip to go straight to the examination.

| Skip | Continue |

The sample questions in the tutorial are unrelated to the exam you are taking. The tutorial will take 10 minutes, and is not included in the test time. The test will only start once you have completed or skipped the tutorial. A screen will appear that gives the exam information (the time, number of questions and name of the exam).

Examination: 6189-21-006 Understand and apply domestic cold water system installation and maintenance techniques

Number of questions: 55

Time allowed: 110 minutes

Note: Examination conditions now apply.

The next screen that will appear is the Help screen, which will give you instructions on how to navigate through this examination. Please click OK to view the Help screen.

The time allowed for the examination will start after you have left the Help screen.

A warning message will appear 5 minutes before the end of the examination.

After clicking 'OK', the Help screen will appear. Clicking the 'Help' button on the toolbar at any time during the exam will recall this screen.

Help Screen

Select your answers from the options displayed. Your answer is stored when you move to another question.

 indicates a selected option. To clear your selection, click the selected option again or select a different option.

Use your mouse to select the command buttons at the top of the screen. Active buttons are bright. If a command button is dim, it is unavailable.

Clicking this...   Does this...

Time
The time remaining is shown in the bottom right-hand corner. Clicking on the icon displays or hides the time.

Help
The Help facility is available throughout the examination.

Review
Displays a window that enables you to review questions already viewed, indicating those answered and marked. To review all items, ensure the 'view marked questions only' checkbox is unchecked. Double-click on the question number to go to the question you want to review.

Mark
Mark flags the current question for review. The button appears light if the question is marked. The question can then be reviewed later by selecting it from the review window.

Clicking this...   Does this...

Previous
Moves you back to the previous question.

Next
Moves you forward to the next question.

Exhibit
Displays a window containing additional information needed to answer the question. Close the 'Exhibit' to return to the question.

Quit
Exits the examination.

OK

After clicking 'OK' while in the Help screen, the exam timer will start and you will see the first question. The question number is always shown in the lower left-hand corner of the screen. If you answer a question but wish to return to it later, then you can click the 'Flag' button. When you get to the end of the test, you can choose to review these flagged questions.

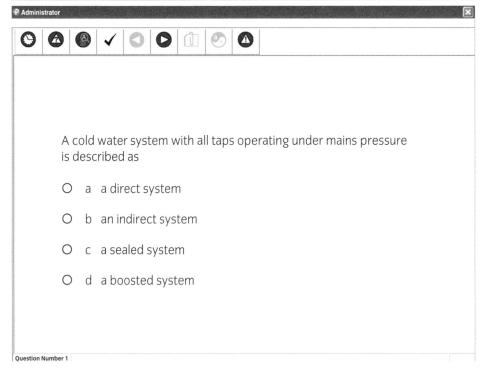

Notes

If you select 'Quit' on the toolbar at any point, you will be given the choice of ending the test. **If you select 'Yes', you will not be able to go back to your test.**

If you click 'Time' on the toolbar at any point, the time that you have left will appear in the bottom right-hand corner. When the exam timer counts down to five minutes, a warning will flash on the screen.

Some of the questions in the test may be accompanied by pictures or diagrams. The question will tell you whether you will need to click on the 'Exhibit' button to view an image.

Notes

When you reach the final question and click 'Next' you will reach a screen that allows you to 'Review your answers' or 'Continue' to end the test. You can review all of your answers or only the ones you have flagged. To review all your answers, make sure that the 'View marked questions only' checkbox is unchecked (click to uncheck). After you have completed your review, you can click 'Continue' to end the test.

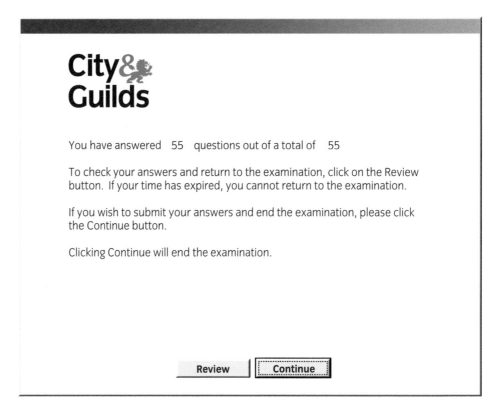

Once you choose to end the exam by clicking 'Continue', the 'Test completed' screen will appear. Click on 'OK' to end the exam.

At the end of the exam, you will be given an 'Examination Score Report'. This gives a provisional grade (pass or fail) and breakdown of score by section. This shows your performance in a bar chart and in percentage terms, which allows you to assess your own strengths and weaknesses. If you did not pass, it gives valuable feedback on which areas of the course you should revise before re-sitting the exam.

Notes

Examination Score Report

Candidate: John Smith

Enrolment No: nav0001

Centre: City & Guilds UK Test Centre 1

Centre No: wow483

Examination: 6189-21-006 Understand and apply domestic cold water system installation and maintenance techniques

Provisional grade: Pass

Breakdown of score by section

Section	Score
01 Know the cold water supply route to dwellings	97%
02 Know the types of cold water system and their layout requirements	89%
03 Know the site preparation techniques for cold water systems and components	85%
04 Know the installation requirements of cold water systems and components	88%
05 Know the service and maintenance requirements of cold water systems and components	86%
06 Know the decommissioning requirements of cold water systems and components	96%
07 Know the inspection and soundness testing requirements of cold water systems and components	91%

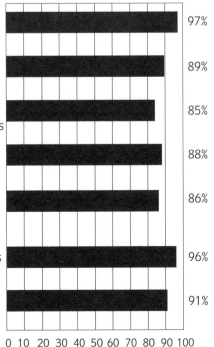

This chart provides feedback to show candidate performance for each section of the test. It should be used along with the Test Specification, which can be found in the Scheme Handbook.

Notes

Frequently asked questions

When can I sit the paper?
You can sit the exam at any time, as there are no set exam dates. You may need to check with your centre when it is able to hold exam sessions.

Can I use any reference books in the test?
Yes, but only normative reference documents in units 006 to 011 only.

How many different knowledge exams are there?
This depends on your qualification route. The Level 2 Plumbing & Heating Diploma (6189-11) route requires completion of 10 knowledge examinations; the Level 2 Domestic Heating Diploma route requires completion of eight knowledge examinations. Each exam is of varying duration.

Do I have a time limit for taking the exams?
Yes, but each exam is of varying duration.

Do I need to be good at IT to do the test online?
No, the system is really easy to use, and you can practise before doing the test.

What happens if the computer crashes in the middle of my test?
This is unlikely, because of the way the system has been designed. If there is some kind of power or system failure, then your answers will be saved and you can continue on another machine if necessary.

Can people hack into the system and cheat?
There are lots of levels of security built into the system to ensure its safety. Also, each person gets a different set of questions, which makes it very difficult to cheat.

Can I change my answers?
Yes, you can change your answers quickly, easily and clearly at any time in the test up to the point where you end the exam. With any answers you feel less confident about, you can click the 'Flag' button, which means you can review these questions before you end the test.

How do I know how long I've got left to complete the test?
You can check the time remaining at any point during the exam by clicking on the 'Time' icon in the toolbar. The time remaining will come up in the bottom right-hand corner of the screen.

Is there only one correct answer (A, B, C or D) to multiple-choice questions?
Yes.

What happens if I don't answer all of the questions?
You should attempt to answer all of the questions. If you find a question difficult, mark it using the 'Flag' button and return to it later.

What grades of pass are there?
You can only achieve either a Pass or a Fail.

When can I re-sit the test if I fail?
You can re-sit the exam at any time, as soon as you and your tutor decide it is right for you, subject to the availability of the online examination.

Notes

Notes

Exam content

To help you to fully understand the exam content, this chapter details the learning outcomes that are assessed in each of the 10 knowledge learning unit areas.

Each individual unit is broken down into one or more learning outcomes. Each learning outcome has a number of assessment criteria (these are the things that you should know to be able to pass the exam). You can find all the assessment criteria in the qualification handbook.

Unit 001
Understand and carry out safe working practices in building services engineering

Notes

Duration
110 mins

Unit aim
The unit provides learning in the essential health and safety job knowledge required to work safely in the Building Services Engineering industries. The essential job knowledge covered relates to work on new-build construction sites (dwellings and industrial/commercial buildings) and refurbishment work in occupied and unoccupied properties (dwellings and industrial/commercial buildings).

Outcome	No. of questions	%
1. Know the health and safety legislation that applies to the building services industry	6	11
2. Know how to recognise and respond to hazardous situations while working in the building services industry	14	25
3. Know the safe personal protection measures while working in the building services industry	3	5
4. Know how to respond to accidents that occur while working in the building services industry	6	11
5. Know the procedures for electrical safety when working in the building services industry	6	11
6. Know the methods of working safely with heat-producing equipment in the building services industry	8	15
7. Know the methods of safely using access equipment in the building services industry	7	13
8. Know the methods of working safely in excavations and confined spaces in the building services industry	5	9
Total	**55**	**100**

Notes

Unit 002
Understand how to communicate with others in building services engineering

Duration
40 mins

Unit aim
The unit provides learning in the development and continued maintenance of effective working relationships in the building services industry associated with work in dwellings, industrial and commercial premises and for private and contract-type clients.

Outcome	No. of questions	%
1. Know the members of the construction team and their role within the building services industry	5	25
2. Know how to apply information sources in the building services industry	9	45
3. Know how to communicate with others in the building services industry	6	30
Total	**20**	**100**

Unit 003
Understand how to apply environmental protection measures within building services engineering

Duration
50 mins

Unit aim
The unit provides learning in a range of basic measures associated with protection of the environment. Areas covered include the effective use of material resources and minimising wastage. The legislation surrounding the effective use of energy and water resources, including an introduction to the use of environmental emerging technologies, is also covered in the unit.

Outcome	No. of questions	%
1. Know the energy conservation legislation that applies to the building services industry	2	8
2. Know the applications of energy sources used in the building services industry	7	28
3. Know the importance of energy conservation when commissioning building services systems	2	8
4. Know the methods of reducing waste and conserving energy while working in the building services industry	3	12
5. Know how to safely dispose of materials used in the building services industry	5	20
6. Know the methods of conserving and reducing wastage of water within the building services industry	6	24
Total	**25**	**100**

Unit 004
Understand how to apply scientific principles within mechanical engineering services

Duration
80 mins

Unit aim
The unit provides learning in the essential scientific principles that underpin the installation, commissioning and maintenance requirements of systems and components in the Mechanical Engineering Services industries. The unit also provides learning in a range of basic calculation methodologies underpinning system and component design.

Outcome	No. of questions	%
1. Know the standard units of measurement used in the mechanical services industry	3	7
2. Know the properties of materials used in the mechanical services industry	17	43
3. Know the relationship between energy, heat and power in the mechanical services industry	6	15
4. Know the principles of pressure and their application in the mechanical services industry	8	20
5. Know simple mechanical principles and their application in the mechanical services industry	2	5
6. Know the principles of electricity as they relate to the mechanical services industry	4	10
Total	**40**	**100**

Unit 005
Understand and carry out site preparation, and pipework fabrication techniques for domestic plumbing and heating systems

Duration
100 mins

Unit aim
The unit provides learning in a range of basic pipework competences that underpin work on plumbing and heating systems. The unit also provides an introduction to the range of work activities carried out in plumbing and heating as well as methods of checking that pipework and plumbing and heating components are leak free.

Outcome	No. of questions	%
1. Know the types of hand and power tools used for domestic plumbing and heating work	9	18
2. Know the types of domestic plumbing and heating pipework and their jointing principles	14	23
3. Know the general site preparation techniques for plumbing and heating work	11	24
4. Know how to use clips and brackets to support domestic plumbing and heating pipework and components	5	11
5. Know the installation requirements of domestic plumbing and heating pipework	8	18
6. Know the inspection and soundness testing requirements of domestic plumbing and heating pipework	3	6
Total	**50**	**100**

Unit 006
Understand and apply domestic cold water system installation and maintenance techniques

Duration
110 mins

Unit aim
The unit provides learning in the installation, maintenance, decommissioning and soundness testing of a basic range of cold water system/component types in dwellings and industrial/commercial properties (of similar size and scope to domestic dwellings). The unit covers systems in buildings up to three storeys in height with pipework up to 28 mm diameter. The scope of the system is from the boundary stop valve into the property feeding the water outlets.

Outcome	No. of questions	%
1. Know the cold water supply route to dwellings	5	9
2. Know the types of cold water system and their layout requirements	15	27
3. Know the site preparation techniques for cold water systems and components	6	11
4. Know the installation requirements of cold water systems and components	13	24
5. Know the service and maintenance requirements of cold water systems and components	6	11
6. Know the decommisioning requirements of cold water systems and components	5	9
7. Know the inspection and soundness testing requirements of cold water systems and components	5	9
Total	**55**	**100**

Unit 007
Understand and apply domestic hot water system installation and maintenance techniques

Duration
120 mins

Unit aim
The unit provides learning in the installation, maintenance, decommissioning and soundness testing of a basic range of hot water system/component types in dwellings and industrial/commercial properties (of similar size and scope to domestic dwellings). The unit covers systems in buildings up to three storeys in height with pipework up to 28 mm diameter.

Outcome	No. of questions	%
1. Know the types of hot water system and their layout requirements	22	37
2. Know the site preparation techniques for hot water systems and components	6	9
3. Know the installation requirements of hot water systems and components	14	25
4. Know the service and maintenance requirements of hot water systems and components	7	11
5. Know the decommissioning requirements of cold water systems and components	5	9
6. Know the inspection and soundness testing requirements of hot water systems and components	6	9
Total	**60**	**100**

Unit 008
Understand and apply domestic central heating system installation and maintenance techniques

Duration
120 mins

Unit aim
The unit provides basic learning in the installation, maintenance, decommissioning and soundness testing of a basic range of wet central heating system/component types in dwellings and industrial/commercial properties (of similar size and scope to domestic dwellings). The unit covers systems in buildings up to three storeys in height and with systems up to a maximum of 40 kW heat output and pipework up to 32 mm diameter. The unit provides an appreciation of the working principles of the various fossil fuel-type heat-producing appliances.

Outcome	No. of questions	%
1. Know the uses of central heating systems in dwellings	3	5
2. Know the types of central heating system and their layout requirements	20	33
3. Know the site preparation techniques for central heating systems and components	6	10
4. Know the installation requirements of central heating systems and components	15	25
5. Know the service and maintenance requirements of central heating systems and components	6	10
6. Know the decommissioning requirements of central heating systems and components	6	10
7. Know the inspection and soundness testing requirements of central heating systems and components	4	7
Total	**60**	**100**

Unit 009
Understand and apply domestic rainwater system installation and maintenance techniques

Duration
70 mins

Unit aim
The unit provides learning in the installation and maintenance of gravity rainwater systems that are installed on dwellings and industrial/commercial properties (of similar size and scope to domestic dwellings) in buildings up to three storeys in height.

Outcome	No. of questions	%
1. Know the general principles of gravity rainwater systems	5	14
2. Know the layout requirements of gravity rainwater systems	9	25
3. Know the site preparation techniques for gravity rainwater systems	7	20
4. Know the installation requirements of gravity rainwater systems	8	23
5. Know the service and maintenance requirements of gravity rainwater systems	3	9
6. Know the inspection and testing requirements of gravity rainwater systems	3	9
Total	**35**	**100**

Unit 010
Understand and apply domestic above-ground drainage system installation and maintenance techniques

Duration
100 mins

Unit aim
The unit provides learning in the installation, maintenance decommissioning and soundness testing of a range of sanitary appliances and connecting sanitary pipework systems in dwellings and industrial/commercial properties (of similar size and scope to domestic dwellings) in buildings up to five storeys in height.

Outcome	No. of questions	%
1. Know the uses of sanitary appliances and their operating principles	4	8
2. Know the types of sanitary pipework system and their layout requirements	17	34
3. Know the site preparation techniques for sanitary appliances and connecting pipework systems	6	12
4. Know the installation requirements of sanitary appliances and connecting pipework systems	9	18
5. Know the service and maintenance requirements of sanitary appliances and connecting pipework systems	5	10
6. Know the decommissioning requirements of sanitary appliances and connecting pipework systems	6	12
7. Know the inspection and soundness testing requirements of sanitary appliances and connecting pipework systems	3	6
Total	**50**	**100**

Tips from the examiner

The following tips are intended to aid confident test performance.

✔ If you rarely use a computer, try to get some practice beforehand. You need to be able to use a mouse to move a cursor arrow around a computer screen, as you will use the cursor to click on the correct answer in the exam.

✔ Make the most of the learning that you will complete before taking the exams. Try to attend all sessions and be prepared to devote time outside the class to revising for the exams.

✔ On the day of the exams, allow plenty of time for travel to the centre and arrive at the place of the exam at least ten minutes before it's due to start so that you have time to relax and get into the right frame of mind.

✔ Listen carefully to the instructions given by the invigilator.

✔ Read the question and every answer before making your selection. Do not rush – there should be plenty of time to answer all the questions.

✔ Look at the exhibits where instructed. Remember, an exhibit supplies you with information that is required to answer the question.

✔ Attempt to answer all the questions. If a question is not answered, it is marked as wrong. Making an educated guess improves your chances of choosing the correct answer. Remember, if you don't select an answer, you will definitely get no marks for that question.

✔ The order of the exam questions follows the order of learning outcomes shown in this publication for each unit. Therefore, look for the answers to early questions at the front of the book and progress through it as you work through the exam questions.

✔ Don't worry about answering the questions in the order in which they appear in the exam. Choose the 'Flag' option on the toolbar to annotate the questions you want to come back to. If you spend too much time on questions early on, you may not have time to answer the later questions, even though you know the answers.

Notes

✔ A basic, non-programmable calculator can be used with the exams so remember to bring it with you.

✔ If you are having trouble finding information in a particular normative document, remember to use the subject index for the document. Using the index should minimise the time it takes you to find the relevant topic.

✔ It is **not** recommended that you memorise any of the material presented here in the hope it will come up in the exam. The exam questions featured in this book will help you to gauge the kinds of questions that might be asked. It is highly unlikely you will be asked any identical questions in the exam, but you may see variations on certain themes.

Understand and carry out site preparation, and pipework fabrication techniques for domestic plumbing and heating systems (6189-005)

6189-005

Notes

Sample test

The sample test below is for paper 6189-005, Understand and carry out site preparation, and pipework fabrication techniques for domestic plumbing and heating systems. The sample test has 30 questions – remember that the actual exam has 50 questions. The test appears first without answers, so you can use it as a mock exam. It is then repeated with answers and explanations. Finally, there is an answer key for easy reference.

Answer the questions by filling in the circle next to your chosen option.

1   What is the name of the tool shown in the diagram?

- ○ a   Basin wrench
- ○ b   'Footprint' wrench
- ○ c   'Stilson' wrench
- ○ d   Torque wrench.

2   Which is the most important item of PPE to wear when using a large hammer drill?

- ○ a   Dust mask
- ○ b   Hi-visibility jacket
- ○ c   Safety goggles
- ○ d   Barrier cream.

3   What is the main safety risk associated with a chisel with a 'mushroomed head'?

- ○ a   Flying steel splinters
- ○ b   Dermatitis
- ○ c   Hearing damage
- ○ d   Tool slippage.

4   Which guard is the main safety feature of a powered circular saw?

- ○ a   Chuck
- ○ b   Blade
- ○ c   Pipe
- ○ d   Fence.

5   Standard copper tube for use in domestic plumbing and heating systems is categorised as

- ○ a   R 220 soft coils
- ○ b   R 220 hard coils
- ○ c   R 250 half-hard lengths
- ○ d   R 290 hard lengths.

6   Which one of the following types of sanitary pipework material can be degraded by ultraviolet (UV) light?

- ○ a   PVC-u
- ○ b   ABS
- ○ c   MDPE
- ○ d   MuPVC.

7   Copper tube used in plumbing and heating systems is available in which one of the following outside diameters?

- ○ a   13 mm
- ○ b   18 mm
- ○ c   24 mm
- ○ d   28 mm.

8   New copper pipe should be jointed to an existing lead supply pipe using a

- ○ a   pressfit fitting
- ○ b   capillary soldered fitting
- ○ c   threaded adaptor fitting
- ○ d   proprietary compression fitting.

Notes

9 **A non-manipulative compression fitting used on copper pipe includes a**

○ a   rubber 'o' ring
○ b   rubber washer
○ c   brass olive
○ d   solder ring.

10 Multiple small-diameter pipes from radiators in a central heating system can be connected to a single central heating main pipe using a

○ a   reducing set
○ b   manifold
○ c   coupling set
○ d   hopper head.

11 What substance is used to aid the flow of solder across the surface of a pipe and the fitting being jointed?

○ a   Putty
○ b   Jointing paste
○ c   Silicone sealant
○ d   Flux.

12 The fitting shown below will be used to joint which pipework material?

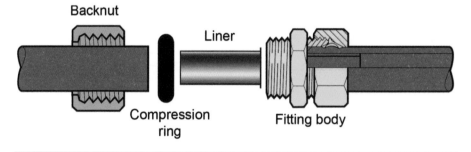

○ a   Copper hot water
○ b   MDPE cold water
○ c   PVC-u waste
○ d   Low carbon steel heating.

13 The bending machine shown in the following diagram is used with which type of pipework?

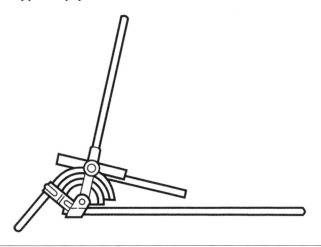

- a Copper
- b Low-carbon steel
- c Stainless steel
- d Polybutylene.

14 Large-radius bends can be successfully made by hand in which one of the following types of copper tube?

- a R290 hard lengths
- b R250 hard lengths
- c R250 half-hard lengths
- d R220 soft coils.

15 Temporary decommissioning can be described as

- a taking a system out of use to work on it
- b completely removing a plumbing or heating system
- c replacing components in a plumbing or heating system
- d calculating the size of pipework and materials in a system.

16 Which one of the following must be handed over to the customer when completing plumbing or heating work?

- a Appliance manufacturer installation/operating instructions
- b Schedule of materials for the work
- c Planning permission application form
- d Qualification certificates for all operatives completing the work.

17 When replacing plumbing components in an airing cupboard that is full of clothes, the best method of avoiding damage to the clothing is to

- a cover it with polythene sheeting
- b ask the customer to remove it from the cupboard
- c cover it with dust sheets
- d check that the customer's insurance will cover any damage.

18 When using a blowtorch to joint capillary-soldered fittings, damage to customer property is most likely to occur due to

- a fire
- b water
- c toxic gas
- d corrosion.

19 On a construction site, heating boilers should normally be stored in

- a the empty house being worked on
- b an open-air compound
- c a locked store in a compound
- d a fully completed house.

20 What is the maximum diameter of hole that can be drilled in a timber first-floor joist with a depth of 150 mm?

- a 12 mm
- b 22 mm
- c 37 mm
- d 57 mm.

21 Under the Building Regulations, what is the maximum permitted depth of vertical chase in a 100 mm deep concrete block?

- ○ a   10 mm
- ○ b   25 mm
- ○ c   33 mm
- ○ d   50 mm.

22 What is the maximum recommended clip spacing distance for horizontal runs of 15 mm polybutylene pipework?

- ○ a   300 mm
- ○ b   500 mm
- ○ c   900 mm
- ○ d   1200 mm.

23 What type of fixing is recommended to secure tongue-and-groove floor boarding that provides access to plumbing or heating pipework?

- ○ a   Nails
- ○ b   Screws
- ○ c   Rubber nut fixings
- ○ d   Coach bolts.

24 Which one of the following is used with a screw to make a fixing into a masonry wall surface?

- ○ a   Cavity fixing
- ○ b   Plastic wall plug
- ○ c   Coach bolt
- ○ d   Nail.

25 A hollow wall cavity fixing is used with which type of wall surface material?

- ○ a   Brick
- ○ b   Concrete block
- ○ c   Timber
- ○ d   Plasterboard.

Notes

Notes

26 Which one of the following types of bracket is suitable for use on low-carbon steel pipework?

- a   Plastic nail type
- b   Plastic stand-off
- c   Copper saddle
- d   Steel munson ring.

27 Copper plumbing and heating pipes should be sleeved when passing through

- a   aluminium framed partition
- b   plasterboard partition walls
- c   kitchen units
- d   load-bearing walls.

28 Which one of the following types of building plans or drawings shows the location of plumbing and heating pipework in the building?

- a   Site plan
- b   Building detail plan
- c   Services drawing
- d   Location drawing.

29 Which one of the following processes would be included in a visual inspection of a pipework system before soundness testing with water?

- a   Check for correct water flow rate
- b   Check to ensure no open ends
- c   Inspect for signs of soapy discharge
- d   Check all insulation has been applied.

30 Water Regulations guidance identifies that cold water pipework is normally tested for soundness using a

- a   multi-meter
- b   hydraulic test kit
- c   manometer
- d   pneumatic test kit.

Questions and answers

The questions for this unit are repeated below with worked-through answers, which where relevant are linked to an appropriate normative reference source.

Knowledge learning outcome 1
Know the types of hand and power tools used for domestic plumbing and heating work

1   **What is the name of the tool shown in the diagram?**

- ○ a   Basin wrench
- ◉ b   'Footprint' wrench
- ○ c   'Stilson' wrench
- ○ d   Torque wrench.

Answer b
Footprint wrenches (option b) as shown in the diagram have drop forged hooks and are fitted to a pressed frame. The teeth are induction hardened to ensure a high grip is maintained. This traditional plumber's tool is an all-purpose wrench, which grips the work piece tighter as more pressure is exerted.

2   **Which is the most important item of PPE to wear when using a large hammer drill?**

- ○ a   Dust mask
- ○ b   Hi-visibility jacket
- ◉ c   Safety goggles
- ○ d   Barrier cream.

Answer c
The greatest risk when using a hammer drill is flying masonry pieces. Because of this, safety goggles are the most important item of PPE.

Notes

3   **What is the main safety risk associated with a chisel with a 'mushroomed head'?**

◉ a   Flying steel splinters
○ b   Dermatitis
○ c   Hearing damage
○ d   Tool slippage.

Answer a
When using a cold chisel that has become 'mushroomed', the thinned metal that forms part of the mushrooming on the head can become dislodged when the chisel is in use, and may possibly cause a severe eye injury to the tool user.

4   **Which guard is the main safety feature of a powered circular saw?**

○ a   Chuck
◉ b   Blade
○ c   Pipe
○ d   Fence.

Answer b
Circular saws all have a blade guard fitted to stop the blade damaging the user; this should never be used during operation.

Knowledge learning outcome 2
Know the types of domestic plumbing and heating pipework and their jointing principles

5   **Standard copper tube for use in domestic plumbing and heating systems is categorised as**

○ a   R 220 soft coils
○ b   R 220 hard coils
◉ c   R 250 half-hard lengths
○ d   R 290 hard lengths.

Notes

Answer c

The types of copper pipe are made in accordance with EN 1057; R250 half-hard lengths is the standard type of copper used in a plumbing or heating system.

Material temper	Lengths supplied (m)	Form of tube delivery	Diameter (mm)	
			from	to
R220 (annealed)	10–50	Coils	6	28
R250 (half-hard)	3–6	Straight lengths	6	267
R290 (hard)	3–6		6	267

6 **Which one of the following types of sanitary pipework material can be degraded by ultraviolet (UV) light?**

○ a   PVC-u
◉ b   ABS
○ c   MDPE
○ d   MuPVC.

Answer b

ABS or acrylonitrile butadiene styrene is often used in solvent-weld waste pipework systems. It has a specific weakness for UV solar radiation and for this reason it is not recommended for external use unless it is painted or boxed in.

7 **Copper tube used in plumbing and heating systems is available in which one of the following outside diameters?**

○ a   13 mm
○ b   18 mm
○ c   24 mm
◉ d   28 mm.

Answer d

The smallest outside-diameter copper tubes for use in the plumbing industry are as follows:

8 mm, 10 mm, 12 mm, 15 mm, 22 mm, 28 mm and 35 mm.

8 **New copper pipe should be jointed to an existing lead supply pipe using a**

○ a   pressfit fitting
○ b   capillary soldered fitting
○ c   threaded adaptor fitting
◉ d   proprietary compression fitting.

Answer d
Lead pipe suffers from not having a uniform profile, making it very hard to connect to with new pipework services. The only method that can make a watertight connection that will not result in lead contamination of the water supply between MDPE or copper pipe and lead pipework is a proprietary compression fitting.

9 **A non-manipulative compression fitting used on copper pipe includes a**

○ a   rubber 'o' ring
○ b   rubber washer
◉ c   brass olive
○ d   solder ring.

Answer c
Non-manipulative compression fittings used on copper pipework come in three parts: a brass body, brass back nut and a brass olive.

10 **Multiple small-diameter pipes from radiators in a central heating system can be connected to a single central heating main pipe using a**

○ a   reducing set
◉ b   manifold
○ c   coupling set
○ d   hopper head.

Answer b
Often mini-bore heating systems use a purpose-made manifold to evenly distribute the heating water from a central point, to save time on installation and help equalise the flow rates to the system's radiators.

11 What substance is used to aid the flow of solder across the surface of a pipe and the fitting being jointed?

- ○ a   Putty
- ○ b   Jointing paste
- ○ c   Silicone sealant
- ◉ d   Flux.

Answer d

Flux is used to prevent oxidation of the two surfaces being soldered during the soldering process. This is to allow the solder to flow between the two surfaces being jointed without sticking, and not flowing on the surfaces being soldered.

12 The fitting shown below will be used to joint which pipework material?

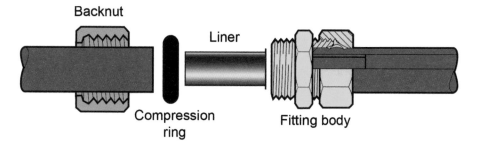

Backnut

Liner

Compression ring

Fitting body

- ○ a   Copper hot water
- ◉ b   MDPE cold water
- ○ c   PVC-u waste
- ○ d   Low carbon steel heating.

Answer b

All of the options use compression fittings, but the picture clearly indicates the use of a pipe stiffener or liner, which shows the material being jointed is not rigid in its own right. This discounts all types of pipework other than MDPE as it is the only type that requires stiffening for compression jointing.

13 The bending machine shown in the following diagram is used with which type of pipework?

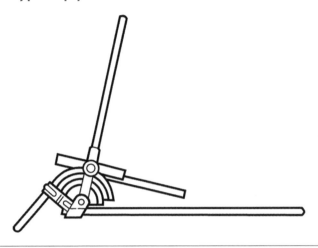

- ⦿ a Copper
- ○ b Low-carbon steel
- ○ c Stainless steel
- ○ d Polybutylene.

Answer a

The only type of pipework that can be bent successfully by a scissor-bending machine is copper pipe.

14 Large-radius bends can be successfully made by hand in which one of the following types of copper tube?

- ○ a R290 hard lengths
- ○ b R250 hard lengths
- ○ c R250 half-hard lengths
- ⦿ d R220 soft coils.

Answer d

Of the types of copper pipe listed – R290 copper (option a) is impossible to bend successfully by machine or by hand, R250 copper (options b and c) can be bent by machine but again not by hand. Only R220 copper (option d) can be manipulated by hand into a large-radius bend successfully.

Knowledge learning outcome 3
Know the general site preparation techniques for plumbing and heating work

15 Temporary decommissioning can be described as

- ◉ a   taking a system out of use to work on it
- ○ b   completely removing a plumbing or heating system
- ○ c   replacing components in a plumbing or heating system
- ○ d   calculating the size of pipework and materials in a system.

Answer a

When you temporarily decommission a plumbing system you take the system out of operation while work is being undertaken (option a) then you re-commission the system back into use when the work is completed. The other options are incorrect; option b is an example of permanent decommissioning, while option c covers system maintenance and option d is a design activity.

16 Which one of the following must be handed over to the customer when completing plumbing or heating work?

- ◉ a   Appliance manufacturer installation/operating instructions
- ○ b   Schedule of materials for the work
- ○ c   Planning permission application form
- ○ d   Qualification certificates for all operatives completing the work.

Answer a

An important part of the commissioning process is the system handover to the customer. This includes a detailed description and demonstration of the system's functions, and a handover of the system's operating instructions and commissioning documentation. The other options detail documentation that is not relevant to the commissioning function.

Notes

17 When replacing plumbing components in an airing cupboard that is full of clothes, the best method of avoiding damage to the clothing is to

○ a   cover it with polythene sheeting
◉ b   ask the customer to remove it from the cupboard
○ c   cover it with dust sheets
○ d   check that the customer's insurance will cover any damage.

Answer b
The best way of ensuring that clothing will not become damaged is to have the customer remove the items before work takes place, as this way any damage is completely avoided. With the other options there is potential for damage to occur to the clothing.

18 When using a blowtorch to joint capillary-soldered fittings, damage to customer property is most likely to occur due to

◉ a   fire
○ b   water
○ c   toxic gas
○ d   corrosion.

Answer a
When soldering, fire damage is a distinct risk. To try to minimise this, fire-resistant materials can be used but this protection is not 100% effective so extreme care still needs to be taken.

19 On a construction site, heating boilers should normally be stored in

○ a   the empty house being worked on
○ b   an open-air compound
◉ c   a locked store in a compound
○ d   a fully completed house.

Answer c
Because of the high value of heating boilers, there is a great need to store them in a secure storage area to prevent theft from site and water damage occurring.

20 What is the maximum diameter of hole that can be drilled in a timber first-floor joist with a depth of 150 mm?

Notes

- ○ a   12 mm
- ○ b   22 mm
- ◉ c   37 mm
- ○ d   57 mm.

Answer c

BS 6700 section 6.1.7.9 – piping passing through structural timbers shall not be notched or bored in such a way that the integrity of the structure is compromised. The maximum size of hole that may be drilled in a timber floor joist is the depth of the joist divided by 4. So if the joist is 150 mm thick the calculation would be 150 mm ÷ 4 = 37 mm.

21 Under the Building Regulations, what is the maximum permitted depth of vertical chase in a 100 mm deep concrete block?

- ○ a   10 mm
- ○ b   25 mm
- ◉ c   33 mm
- ○ d   50 mm.

Answer c

The Building Regulations Approved Document A section 2C30 states that any vertical chase in a wall can be up to one third of the thickness of the wall, and any horizontal chase can but up to one sixth of the wall thickness. So if the wall is 100 mm thick the calculation would be 100 mm ÷ 3 = 33 mm.

Knowledge learning outcome 4
Know how to use clips and brackets to support domestic plumbing and heating pipework and components

22 What is the maximum recommended clip spacing distance for horizontal runs of 15 mm polybutylene pipework?

- ◉ a   300 mm
- ○ b   500 mm
- ○ c   900 mm
- ○ d   1200 mm.

Notes

Answer a

BS 6700 section 6.1.7.2 (Table 12) identifies that 15 mm polybutylene pipework run horizontally requires clips at a maximum of 300 mm spacings.

23 What type of fixing is recommended to secure tongue-and-groove floor boarding that provides access to plumbing or heating pipework?

- ○ a   Nails
- ◉ b   Screws
- ○ c   Rubber nut fixings
- ○ d   Coach bolts.

Answer b

For maintenance purposes access to pipework should be readily available. Screws are the best method of allowing access to areas that conceal pipework as the possibility of damage to the boards is minimised. Nail fixings would require the use of a nail bar with the possibility of damage to surrounding boards.

24 Which one of the following is used with a screw to make a fixing into a masonry wall surface?

- ○ a   Cavity fixing
- ◉ b   Plastic wall plug
- ○ c   Coach bolt
- ○ d   Nail.

Answer b

Plastic wall plugs are used in conjunction with screws to make solid fixings in brick and masonry.

25 A hollow wall cavity fixing is used with which type of wall surface material?

- ○ a   Brick
- ○ b   Concrete block
- ○ c   Timber
- ◉ d   Plasterboard.

Answer d
Plasterboard, when laid on dabs or on laths, always has a hollow void behind it, requiring the use of a hollow wall fixing to secure plumbing fittings.

26 Which one of the following types of bracket is suitable for use on low-carbon steel pipework?

○ a   Plastic nail type
○ b   Plastic stand-off
○ c   Copper saddle
◉ d   Steel munson ring.

Answer d
Plastic nails in brackets (option a) and plastic stand-off brackets (option b) do not have the strength to hold low-carbon steel pipe securely, and copper saddle clips are not normally sized correctly for steel pipework. Munson ring brackets (option d) offer the best support for low-carbon steel pipework as they have the required strength to support the weight of steel pipework and fittings.

Knowledge learning outcome 5
Know the installation requirements of domestic plumbing and heating pipework

27 Copper plumbing and heating pipes should be sleeved when passing through

○ a   aluminium framed partition
○ b   plasterboard partition walls
○ c   kitchen units
◉ d   load-bearing walls.

Answer d
Sleeving is always required for pipework passing through load-bearing walls in buildings (option d). The other options are all examples of non-load-bearing structures.

Notes

28 Which one of the following types of building plans or drawings shows the location of plumbing and heating pipework in the building?

○ a   Site plan
○ b   Building detail plan
◉ c   Services drawing
○ d   Location drawing.

Answer c
The services drawing gives details of all the electrical, plumbing and heating layouts for a particular building. The remaining plans or drawing types do not feature details of the services installation.

Knowledge learning outcome 6
Know the inspection and soundness testing requirements of domestic plumbing and heating pipework

29 Which one of the following processes would be included in a visual inspection of a pipework system before soundness testing with water?

○ a   Check for correct water flow rate
◉ b   Check to ensure no open ends
○ c   Inspect for signs of soapy discharge
○ d   Check all insulation has been applied.

Answer b
The visual inspection process has the following checks as part of the inspection.

Check to ensure that:
– the pipework is correctly supported
– all joints have been correctly made and there are no open ends
– the installation meets the requirements of the Building and Water Regulations.

30 Water Regulations guidance identifies that cold water pipework is normally tested for soundness using a

○ a   multi-meter
◉ b   hydraulic test kit
○ c   manometer
○ d   pneumatic test kit.

Answer b

A multi-meter (option a) is used to test electrical circuits. A manometer (option c) is used to test gas or sanitary pipework installations. A pneumatic test kit (option d) is used to air-test installations; air tests are not normally recommended for cold water installations. Cold water pipework is tested using a hydraulic test kit (option b) – this kit incorporates a pump and a pressure gauge to allow the test to be carried out correctly.

Notes

Answer key

Sample test 6189-005

Question	Answer	Question	Answer
1	b	16	a
2	c	17	b
3	a	18	a
4	b	19	c
5	c	20	c
6	b	21	c
7	d	22	a
8	d	23	b
9	c	24	b
10	b	25	d
11	d	26	d
12	b	27	d
13	a	28	c
14	d	29	b
15	a	30	b

Understand and apply domestic cold water system installation and maintenance techniques (6189-006)

6189-006

Notes

Sample test

The sample test below is for paper 6189-006, Understand and apply domestic cold water system installation and maintenance techniques. The sample test has 30 questions – remember that the actual exam has 55 questions. The test appears first without answers, so you can use it as a mock exam. It is then repeated with answers and explanations. Finally, there is an answer key for easy reference.

Answer the questions by filling in the circle next to your chosen option.

1   Which one of the following is an underground water source?

- ○ a   Lake
- ○ b   River
- ○ c   Borehole
- ○ d   Stream.

2   Water to a farmhouse supplied from a moorland collection tank can be identified as

- ○ a   a mains supply
- ○ b   a private supply
- ○ c   a public supply
- ○ d   a multi-purpose supply.

3   Which one of the following must only be provided from a wholesome water source?

- ○ a   Drinking water
- ○ b   WC flushing water
- ○ c   Garden irrigation water
- ○ d   Washing machine water.

4   What is the minimum dimension (shown as X) to the outer
    wall surface in the following diagram of a supply pipe entering
    through a solid floor into a property?

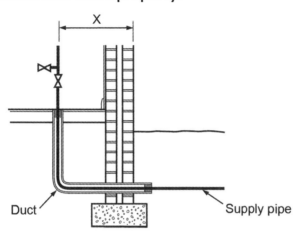

- ○ a   250 mm
- ○ b   400 mm
- ○ c   750 mm
- ○ d   900 mm.

5   What is the name of the cold water system shown in the
    following diagram?

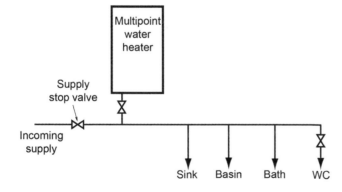

- ○ a   Pressurised system
- ○ b   Indirect system
- ○ c   Direct system
- ○ d   Sealed system.

6 An indirect cold water system is most likely to be selected when

○ a   there is a high incoming mains flow rate
○ b   there is a low incoming mains flow rate
○ c   a reduction in system pipework is required
○ d   water storage needs to be kept to a minimum.

7 What is the minimum recommended size of a cold water distributing pipe feeding a bath tap outlet in an indirect cold water system?

○ a   10 mm
○ b   15 mm
○ c   22 mm
○ d   28 mm.

8 Which one of the following provides protection against backflow at a wash hand basin tap in a dwelling?

○ a   A service valve
○ b   An air gap
○ c   A single-check valve
○ d   A pressure-relief valve.

9 Component X in the following diagram is a

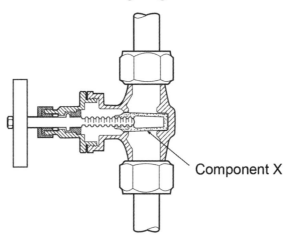

Component X

○ a   rubber washer
○ b   wedge-shaped gate
○ c   ceramic disc
○ d   fibre washer.

10 Which one of the following must be fitted to the overflow (warning pipe) in a protected cold water storage cistern?

○ a   Insect screen

○ b   Double check valve

○ c   Service valve

○ d   Baffle plate.

11 Which British Standard details the type of pipework materials that can be used in a cold water system?

○ a   BS 5440

○ b   BS 6700

○ c   BS EN 12056

○ d   BS EN 12983.

12 Which one of the following health and safety dangers is most likely to be present when using dust sheets as a protective walkway on a laminated timber floor surface?

○ a   Dirt penetration through the sheets

○ b   Slippage of the sheets on the floor surface

○ c   Fire risk due to contact of the flammable materials

○ d   Toxic smells due to contact of the two materials.

13 Which one of the following jointing methods can be used on underground MDPE cold water service pipework?

○ a   Capillary solder ring

○ b   Compression

○ c   Pressfit

○ d   Capillary end feed.

14 Which one of the following would normally be used to tighten a tap connector to a bath pillar tap?

○ a   Screwdriver

○ b   Box spanner

○ c   Basin wrench

○ d   Stilson wrench.

Notes

Notes

15 Which one of the following is an unsuitable type of joint to be used on cold water pipework?

- ○ a   Lead wiped joint
- ○ b   Lead proprietary joint
- ○ c   Pushfit joint
- ○ d   Capillary joint.

16 The Water Regulations state that a service valve must be fitted before

- ○ a   a single check valve
- ○ b   a bath tap outlet
- ○ c   a sink tap outlet
- ○ d   a water heater inlet.

17 Which one of the following should be used to make a hole in a plastic feed and expansion cistern?

- ○ a   Pad saw
- ○ b   Heated copper tube
- ○ c   Hole saw
- ○ d   Heated compression fitting.

18 Which one of the following requirements should be applied to a cold water distributing pipe, laid in a sleeve, in a solid floor without an accessible cover?

- ○ a   The pipe must be capable of being easily withdrawn for repair or renewal
- ○ b   The pipe must be fitted with trace heating to guard against freezing
- ○ c   The sleeve must be fitted with a connection to the drain
- ○ d   The sleeve must feature a self-collapsing design.

19 Which one of the following is normally required when fixing sink pillar taps to a stainless steel sink top?

- ○ a   Top-hat washers
- ○ b   Silicone sealant
- ○ c   Putty and jointing paste
- ○ d   Fibre washers.

20 When making a capillary-soldered tee joint to an existing painted copper pipe the

Notes

- a   paint must be removed from the pipe after jointing
- b   olives should be expanded before the joint is made
- c   paint must be removed from the pipe before jointing
- d   'o' ring must be fully lubricated in order to pass the paint.

21 A cistern is insulated in a building with a 'warm roof' to provide protection against

- a   freezing
- b   corrosion
- c   the growth of legionella bacteria
- d   the production of salmonella bacteria.

22 Which one of the following would normally form part of a routine maintenance inspection (periodic service) of a cold water system?

- a   The replacement of pipework clips and brackets
- b   The opening/closing of service valves to check for correct operation
- c   The opening/closing of double-check valves to check for correct operation
- d   The replacement of plastic cold water storage cisterns.

23 'White dots' on the outside surface of a galvanised cold water storage cistern are a sign of

- a   corrosion
- b   hard water
- c   contamination
- d   pure water.

24 Which one of the following is most likely to be listed in the schedule of activities to be carried out on a cold water system maintenance record?

- a   Check/adjustment of the water level in cisterns
- b   Replacement of the olives in compression fittings
- c   Replacement of the gate mechanism in fullway gate valves
- d   Check/adjustment of disinfectant level in the system.

Notes

25 Which one of the following could be used when connecting an outside tap into an existing cold water supply pipe when the stop valve fails to isolate the supply?

- a   Hydraulic test kit
- b   Backflow prevention device
- c   Float-operated valve
- d   Pipe freezing kit.

26 The cold water supply to a wash hand basin fed from an indirect cold water system is normally isolated at the

- a   service valve on the distributing pipe from the cold water storage cistern
- b   service valve on the cold feed pipe to the hot water storage cylinder
- c   supply stop valve under the kitchen sink
- d   stop valve to the WC flushing cistern.

27 The main risk when leaving open pipe ends connected to a 'live' cold water system when work is taking place is

- a   flooding
- b   fire
- c   theft
- d   contamination.

28 A visual inspection of a cold water system is normally carried out

- a   after filling but before soundness-testing a system
- b   after soundness-testing a system
- c   before filling a system
- d   before soundness-testing but after performance-testing a system.

29 Which one of the following can be used to establish the soundness test pressure in a cold water system?

- a   Pipe freezing kit
- b   Manometer
- c   Multi-meter
- d   Hydraulic test kit.

30 Which one of the following could be the possible cause of a vibration noise heard from the pipework near to a cold water storage cistern?

- ○ a   Poorly supported pipework
- ○ b   Very hard water
- ○ c   Badly corroded pipework
- ○ d   Lack of earth protection.

Notes

Notes

Questions and answers

The questions for this unit are repeated below with worked-through answers, which where relevant are linked to an appropriate normative reference source.

Knowledge learning outcome 1
Know the cold water supply route to dwellings

1 **Which one of the following is an underground water source?**

○ a   Lake
○ b   River
◉ c   Borehole
○ d   Stream.

Answer c
Options a, b and d are all above-ground sources of water. Option c is a type of well, which draws water from below ground.

2 **Water to a farmhouse supplied from a moorland collection tank can be identified as**

○ a   a mains supply
◉ b   a private supply
○ c   a public supply
○ d   a multi-purpose supply.

Answer b
Options c and d are incorrect definitions of water supply methods.

Mains supply – this type of water supply comes directly from the water undertaker via a common supply network as defined under the water industry act 1991.

Private supply – water collected for use from a source that is not supplied from the water undertaker is known as a private water supply.

Notes

3 Which one of the following must only be provided from a wholesome water source?

⦿ a   Drinking water
○ b   WC flushing water
○ c   Garden irrigation water
○ d   Washing machine water.

Answer a

The Building Regulations Approved Document G 2010, G1.1 (a) states that all drinking water draw-off points must be supplied only from a wholesome water source. The same regulations also state that options b, c and d can be supplied from an unwholesome water source such as recycled rainwater and grey water as long as it is of a suitable quality and an appropriate risk assessment has been carried out.

Knowledge learning outcome 2
Know the types of cold water system and their layout requirements

4 What is the minimum dimension (shown as X) to the outer wall surface in the following diagram of a supply pipe entering through a solid floor into a property?

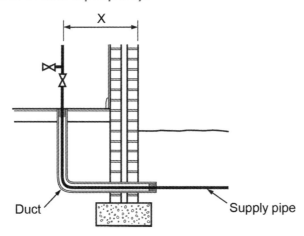

○ a   250 mm
○ b   400 mm
⦿ c   750 mm
○ d   900 mm.

Notes

Answer c

Part 7.3 of Schedule 2 of the Water Supply (Water Fittings) Regulations, specifies a minimum depth of cover of 750 mm for any water fitting laid below ground level to prevent freezing of the water fittings, regardless of direction or orientation of the pipe run.

5   **What is the name of the cold water system shown in the following diagram?**

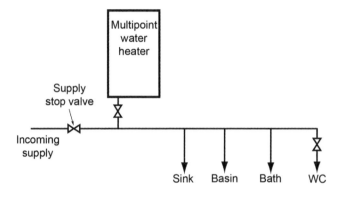

○ a   Pressurised system
○ b   Indirect system
◉ c   Direct system
○ d   Sealed system.

Answer c

Options a and d are not used to define cold water system types but are used in relation to other water systems. The drawing shows an example of a direct water system.

Indirect systems – normally all but the main drinking water point in the system have water supplied from a storage cistern via distributing pipes.

Direct systems – all water draw-off points are fed directly from the supply pipe with no water storage.

6   **An indirect cold water system is most likely to be selected when**

○ a   there is a high incoming mains flow rate
◉ b   there is a low incoming mains flow rate
○ c   a reduction in system pipework is required
○ d   water storage needs to be kept to a minimum.

Answer b
One of the main reasons to select an indirect cold water system, in the place of a direct cold water system, is that the incoming water flow rate form the mains cannot serve the water appliances connected to the system sufficiently.

7 **What is the minimum recommended size of a cold water distributing pipe feeding a bath tap outlet in an indirect cold water system?**

- ○ a   10 mm
- ○ b   15 mm
- ◉ c   22 mm
- ○ d   28 mm.

Answer c
BS 6700 Table 3 recommends that a minimum flow rate of 0.2L/s be supplied to baths as a minimum. It is industry practice to install a 22 mm pipe in an indirect cold water system in a small single-family dwelling, in the place of conducting a complex pipe sizing calculation to ensure this flow rate is achieved.

8 **Which one of the following provides protection against backflow at a wash hand basin tap in a dwelling?**

- ○ a   A service valve
- ◉ b   An air gap
- ○ c   A single-check valve
- ○ d   A pressure-relief valve.

Answer b
The Water Supply (Water Fittings) Regulations require basins to incorporate a protection method against backflow. Options a and d are not recognised as offering any backflow protection. Option c only offers insufficient protection. Option b offers the recognised 25 mm air gap, which grants the required level of backflow prevention required by the regulations.

Notes

9 Component X in the following diagram is a

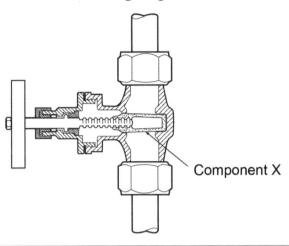

Component X

- ○ a   rubber washer
- ⦿ b   wedge-shaped gate
- ○ c   ceramic disc
- ○ d   fibre washer.

Answer b

Options a and c cannot make up part of the component pictured.

Option d can make up part of the valve head assembly but not the valve body. Option b is the only component listed that forms part of the valve body, as laid out in BS 5154.

10 **Which one of the following must be fitted to the overflow (warning pipe) in a protected cold water storage cistern?**

- ⦿ a   Insect screen
- ○ b   Double check valve
- ○ c   Service valve
- ○ d   Baffle plate.

Answer a

There is a number of mandatory requirements for cold water storage cisterns as laid out clearly in BS 6700 5.2.3.1.2. The overflow (warning) pipe must have provision for the exclusion of insects.

Knowledge learning outcome 3
Know the site preparation techniques for cold water systems and components

11 **Which British Standard details the type of pipework materials that can be used in a cold water system?**

- ○ a   BS 5440
- ◉ b   BS 6700
- ○ c   BS EN 12056
- ○ d   BS EN 12983.

Answer b

Option a, BS 5440, is the standard for flueing and ventilation for gas appliances.

Option c, BS EN 12056, is the standard for gravity drainage systems inside buildings.

Option d, BS EN 12983, is the standard for domestic cookware for use on top of a stove, cooker or hob.

BS 6700 is the standard for design, installation, testing and maintenance of services supplying water for domestic use within buildings and their curtilages. The specification outlining the types of pipework materials that can be used is detailed in Section 4 of the standard.

12 **Which one of the following health and safety dangers is most likely to be present when using dust sheets as a protective walkway on a laminated timber floor surface?**

- ○ a   Dirt penetration through the sheets
- ◉ b   Slippage of the sheets on the floor surface
- ○ c   Fire risk due to contact of the flammable materials
- ○ d   Toxic smells due to contact of the two materials.

Answer b

The nature of laminate floors is that toxic smells cannot occur as the two material types will not react that way (option d); there is no rise in fire risk from the use of dust sheets with laminate flooring (option c); and laminate flooring will not cause greater dirt penetration through the sheets (option a). However, it will affect the traction of the dust sheet to the flooring making slippage a much higher probability (option b).

Notes

13 Which one of the following jointing methods can be used on underground MDPE cold water service pipework?

○ a   Capillary solder ring
◉ b   Compression
○ c   Pressfit
○ d   Capillary end feed.

Answer b
Medium density polyethylene (MDPE) plastic pipe cannot be soldered (options a and d); pressfit (option c) is also not a suitable option for jointing MDPE pipework. Compression fittings (option b) are, however, used extensively on underground MDPE water pipework.

14 Which one of the following would normally be used to tighten a tap connector to a bath pillar tap?

○ a   Screwdriver
○ b   Box spanner
◉ c   Basin wrench
○ d   Stilson wrench.

Answer c
Tap connectors are hexagonal fittings that have no screw head (option a) and tend to be fitted in confined spaces meaning that the use of normal tools such as Stilsons and grips is not possible (option d). A box spanner is not capable of tightening a tap connector to a tap as the pipework would not allow the tool to function (option b). The specific design of the basin wrench allows its use in confined spaces and with pipework connected (option c).

Knowledge learning outcome 4
Know the installation requirements of cold water systems and components

15 Which one of the following is an unsuitable type of joint to be used on cold water pipework?

◉ a   Lead wiped joint
○ b   Lead proprietary joint
○ c   Pushfit joint
○ d   Capillary joint.

Notes

Answer a

BS 6700 Section 4 specifically states that the use of any pipework jointing method that would introduce new lead material into the cold water supply pipework should not be used, including jointing to existing lead pipework. By their nature of jointing, pushfit joints (option c) and proprietary joints (option b) add no new material to the pipework system other than the body of the fitting. Capillary soldering (option d), when used on cold water pipework, is performed with copper/tin (lead free) solder. Lead wiping (option a) of lead pipework does add new lead material to the cold water pipework and because of this may not be performed.

16 The Water Regulations state that a service valve must be fitted before

- ○ a   a single check valve
- ○ b   a bath tap outlet
- ○ c   a sink tap outlet
- ◉ d   a water heater inlet.

Answer d

The Water Supply (Water Fittings) Regulations Schedule 2 Section 11 requires that servicing valves be fitted to minimise water wastage when replacing or maintaining water fittings. Option a would not require a servicing valve to be fitted for maintenance purposes.

Although good practice, it is not mandatory to fit servicing valves to the outlets from sanitary appliances (options b and c), but it is mandatory to fit a servicing valve on water fittings that will require regular maintenance, such water softeners, boilers and water heaters (option d).

17 Which one of the following should be used to make a hole in a plastic feed and expansion cistern?

- ○ a   Pad saw
- ○ b   Heated copper tube
- ◉ c   Hole saw
- ○ d   Heated compression fitting.

Notes

Answer c

When dressing a plastic cistern ready for installation, the method of making holes for the float-operated valve, warning pipe, vent pipe and cold-feed pipework should not be made by using heated pipe or fittings to 'melt' a hole into the cistern (options b and d) as this degrades the strength of the surrounding plastic. Although possible, it is not good practice to use a pad saw to cut the holes into a cistern (option a) as this often results in misshapen and poorly fitting holes for fittings to be dressed into. The correct method is to use a hole saw sized appropriately to the fitting being dressed into the cistern (option c).

18 **Which one of the following requirements should be applied to a cold water distributing pipe, laid in a sleeve, in a solid floor without an accessible cover?**

- ⦿ a The pipe must be capable of being easily withdrawn for repair or renewal
- ○ b The pipe must be fitted with trace heating to guard against freezing
- ○ c The sleeve must be fitted with a connection to the drain
- ○ d The sleeve must feature a self-collapsing design.

Answer a

The Water Supply (Water Fittings) Regulations guidance document for Schedule 2 Section 7 requires that any pipework placed within a solid floor must be able to be removed for inspection, repair or replacement purposes (option a). This means that no self-anchoring fixtures, such as elbows, bends or branches, can be incorporated into the pipe run, unless the duct/sleeve has a removable cover.

19 **Which one of the following is normally required when fixing sink pillar taps to a stainless steel sink top?**

- ⦿ a Top-hat washers
- ○ b Silicone sealant
- ○ c Putty and jointing paste
- ○ d Fibre washers.

Answer a
When fixing taps to a sink top it is often required to give the taps greater stability than other sanitary appliances, due to the thin nature of the steel. Top-hat washers (option a) give the back nut of the tap a much larger surface area and promote tap stability. Silicone sealant and putty and jointing paste (options b and c) should not be used as they do not add to the strength of the joint or stability of the fixing. Fibre washers (option d) are used to make connections between taps and tap connectors but not between taps and the sink top itself.

20 When making a capillary-soldered tee joint to an existing painted copper pipe the

○ a   paint must be removed from the pipe after jointing
○ b   olives should be expanded before the joint is made
◉ c   paint must be removed from the pipe before jointing
○ d   'o' ring must be fully lubricated in order to pass the paint.

Answer c
When making capillary-soldered joints on copper pipework it is important that the surfaces of the pipe and the fitting are clean and free from debris and dirt. Paint should be considered 'dirt' for the process of soldering, and should be removed before the jointing process can be undertaken (option c).

21 A cistern is insulated in a building with a 'warm roof' to provide protection against

○ a   freezing
○ b   corrosion
◉ c   the growth of legionella bacteria
○ d   the production of salmonella bacteria.

Answer c
The Water Supply (Water Fittings) Regulations Schedule 2 Section 16.4 requires that storage cisterns be insulated to stop undue warming, which would result in the growth of bacteria, and to minimise the chances of freezing. The insulation would not cause corrosion of the cistern (option b) and the warm roof space would not be used to protect the cistern from freezing (option a); the insulation would be used to prevent the growth of bacteria (option c).

Notes

Notes

Knowledge learning outcome 5
Know the service and maintenance requirements of cold water systems and components

22 Which one of the following would normally form part of a routine maintenance inspection (periodic service) of a cold water system?

- ○ a   The replacement of pipework clips and brackets
- ◉ b   The opening/closing of service valves to check for correct operation
- ○ c   The opening/closing of double-check valves to check for correct operation
- ○ d   The replacement of plastic cold water storage cisterns.

Answer b
When undertaking routine maintenance on a small cold water system, the only option that would be undertaken from those listed would be the inspection for correct operation of servicing valves (option b). The other options (a, c and d) would require major works to partially dismantle and reassemble the system, which would be beyond what is included in a routine maintenance inspection.

23 'White dots' on the outside surface of a galvanised cold water storage cistern are a sign of

- ◉ a   corrosion
- ○ b   hard water
- ○ c   contamination
- ○ d   pure water.

Answer a
Corrosion in a galvanised steel cold water storage cistern is minimised by applying a zinc coating to the cistern wall surfaces, but as they age the resistance to corrosion breaks down. On the internal surface the steel begins to break down; the corrosion slowly moves towards the external surface. The zinc oxidises into a white/light grey colour, in patches or spots where the steel has become corroded and damaged.

24 Which one of the following is most likely to be listed in the schedule of activities to be carried out on a cold water system maintenance record?

- ⦿ a Check/adjustment of the water level in cisterns
- ○ b Replacement of the olives in compression fittings
- ○ c Replacement of the gate mechanism in fullway gate valves
- ○ d Check/adjustment of disinfectant level in the system.

Answer a

When planning a routine maintenance schedule on a small cold water system, the action that would be listed as part of the inspection activities would be to check for the correct water level in the storage cisterns (option a). Option c would not be undertaken as part of any routine maintenance activity as it is a major repair activity to a valve. Option b is not a repair or maintenance activity that is ever undertaken. Option d is only undertaken as part of a system disinfection procedure listed in BS 6700.

Knowledge learning outcome 6
Know the decommissioning requirements of cold water systems and components

25 Which one of the following could be used when connecting an outside tap into an existing cold water supply pipe when the stop valve fails to isolate the supply?

- ○ a Hydraulic test kit
- ○ b Backflow prevention device
- ○ c Float-operated valve
- ⦿ d Pipe freezing kit.

Answer d

To fully isolate a cold water branch when the supply stop valve fails to function involves using a device or method to stop the flow of water to the area you are going to be working on. Option a is a device used to soundness-test water systems and would not stop the flow of water to a working area. Option b would prevent backflow but not prevent outflow and would not isolate the pipework in any way. Option c would not isolate the supply pipework. Option d would allow the pipework system to be temporarily isolated to allow works to be carried out.

26 The cold water supply to a wash hand basin fed from an indirect cold water system is normally isolated at the

- ⦿ a service valve on the distributing pipe from the cold water storage cistern
- ◯ b service valve on the cold feed pipe to the hot water storage cylinder
- ◯ c supply stop valve under the kitchen sink
- ◯ d stop valve to the WC flushing cistern.

Answer a

On an indirect cold water system where there is not an isolation valve fitted at the appliance, the method of isolation is to turn off the service valve supplying water to the basin from the cold water storage cistern (option a). None of the other options would isolate the cold water supply to the basin.

27 The main risk when leaving open pipe ends connected to a 'live' cold water system when work is taking place is

- ⦿ a flooding
- ◯ b fire
- ◯ c theft
- ◯ d contamination.

Answer a

The main risk when working on a live cold water system is the chance of accidental flooding from open ends (option a). There is a very small risk of contamination (option d) and no risk of fire (option b) or theft (option c).

Knowledge learning outcome 7
Know the inspection and soundness testing requirements of cold water systems and components

28 A visual inspection of a cold water system is normally carried out

- ◯ a after filling but before soundness-testing a system
- ◯ b after soundness-testing a system
- ⦿ c before filling a system
- ◯ d before soundness-testing but after performance-testing a system.

Answer c

The order for soundness-testing a cold water system is shown below:

1) Visual inspection of the system for correct jointing, installation and compliance with regulations and standards
2) Fill the system with water and check for leaks
3) Soundness-test the system at 150% working pressure for 60 minutes
4) Flush the system with wholesome water.

29 Which one of the following can be used to establish the soundness test pressure in a cold water system?

- ○ a Pipe freezing kit
- ○ b Manometer
- ○ c Multi-meter
- ◉ d Hydraulic test kit.

Answer d

Option d is the equipment used to pump a system to the correct test pressure and monitor the pressure level during the test. Option b is used to take pressure readings but at a much lower level than is usually required for a cold water system soundness test. Option a is equipment used for repair and maintenance work and is not used in any way for testing. Option c is used to undertake electrical testing.

30 Which one of the following could be the possible cause of a vibration noise heard from the pipework near to a cold water storage cistern?

- ◉ a Poorly supported pipework
- ○ b Very hard water
- ○ c Badly corroded pipework
- ○ d Lack of earth protection.

Answer a

Vibration noise is often caused because of pipe movement. A lack of proper support would allow excessive movement of pipework and could result in vibration noises from a cold water system.

Notes

Answer key

Sample test 6189-006

Question	Answer	Question	Answer
1	c	16	d
2	b	17	c
3	a	18	a
4	c	19	a
5	c	20	c
6	b	21	c
7	c	22	b
8	b	23	a
9	b	24	a
10	a	25	d
11	b	26	a
12	b	27	a
13	b	28	c
14	c	29	d
15	a	30	a

Understand and apply domestic hot water system installation and maintenance techniques (6189-007)

6189-007

Sample test

The sample test below is for paper 6189-007, Understand and apply domestic hot water system installation and maintenance techniques. The sample test has 30 questions – remember that the actual exam has 60 questions. The test appears first without answers, so you can use it as a mock exam. It is then repeated with answers and explanations. Finally, there is an answer key for easy reference.

Answer the questions by filling in the circle next to your chosen option.

1   What type of hot water system is shown in the following diagram?

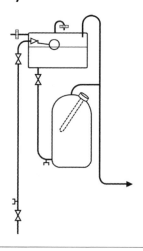

- ○ a   Single-feed indirect system
- ○ b   Double-feed indirect system
- ○ c   Direct system
- ○ d   Point of use system.

2 The lever-operated spherical plug valve shown below uses which one of the following to isolate the water supply?

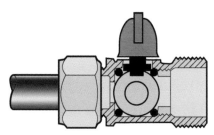

○ a Rubber washer
○ b Ceramic disc
○ c Rotating ball
○ d Gate-shaped wedge.

3 What is the minimum size of an open-vent pipe from a direct hot water storage system?

○ a 28 mm
○ b 22 mm
○ c 15 mm
○ d 10 mm.

4 The expanded water from an indirect open-vented hot water system should travel through which pipe to the feed and expansion cistern?

○ a Primary open vent
○ b Primary cold feed
○ c Secondary open vent
○ d Secondary cold feed.

5 What is the minimum recommended distance that the base to a feed and expansion cistern should project past the edges of the cistern itself?

○ a 50 mm
○ b 100 mm
○ c 150 mm
○ d 250 mm.

6   In comparison to a standard indirect cylinder, a super-duty indirect hot water storage cylinder features a

- ○ a   higher water capacity
- ○ b   lower water capacity
- ○ c   faster heat recovery rate
- ○ d   lower heat recovery rate.

7   A multipoint instantaneous water heater is most suited to providing hot water to

- ○ a   an electric shower
- ○ b   the outlets in a property with one bathroom
- ○ c   the outlets in a property with two bathrooms
- ○ d   the outlets in a property with three bathrooms.

8   The hot water outlet from a multipoint water heater serving a small domestic property is usually sized at

- ○ a   10 mm
- ○ b   15 mm
- ○ c   22 mm
- ○ d   28 mm.

9   In addition to a control thermostat, a new immersion heater must include which one of the following?

- ○ a   A temperature-relief valve
- ○ b   An overheat thermostat
- ○ c   A pressure-relief valve
- ○ d   A double check valve.

10 Backflow is most likely to occur in a hot water system when

- ○ a   a tap outlet discharges below the spillover level of a sanitary appliance
- ○ b   a tap outlet discharges above the spillover level of a sanitary appliance
- ○ c   the water pressure in the hot water system is too great
- ○ d   the water flow rate in the hot water system is too great.

11 A shower mixer valve that operates based on the head of water available between the shower head and base of the storage cistern is known as a

○ a pumped shower with single impellor
○ b pumped shower with twin impellor
○ c gravity-fed shower
○ d mains-fed shower.

12 The Water Regulations state that uninsulated hot water pipework must not be embedded in

○ a chases in external masonry walls
○ b an accessible pipe duct
○ c timber stud partition walls
○ d an accessible pipe chase.

13 Which one of the following types of valves is suitable for use on the cold feed pipe from a storage cistern to a hot water storage cylinder?

○ a Temperature-relief valve
○ b Double check valve
○ c Screwdown stop valve
○ d Fullway gate valve.

14 Which one of the following is normally used to make a watertight seal between a tank connector and a plastic feed and expansion cistern?

○ a Plastic washers
○ b Silicone sealant
○ c Jointing paste
○ d Fibre washers.

15 The water flow rate from outlets in a hot water system can be measured using which one of the following?

○ a Pressure gauge
○ b Weir gauge or flow cup
○ c Multi-meter
○ d Hygrometer.

Notes

Notes

16 Which of the following is true when routing polybutylene pipe through timber first floor joists?

- ○ a Sufficient space must be provided for thermal movement
- ○ b The pipework must be insulated to guard against fire
- ○ c The pipework sections must be connected to the electrical earth
- ○ d Barrier pipe must be used to guard against acid attack from the joists.

17 An uninsulated 22 mm hot water pipe (dead leg) from a hot water cylinder should be no longer than

- ○ a 3 m
- ○ b 6 m
- ○ c 9 m
- ○ d 12 m.

18 The inlet supply to a feed and expansion cistern is controlled by a

- ○ a double check valve
- ○ b temperature-relief valve
- ○ c float-operated valve
- ○ d pressure-reducing valve.

19 The cold feed pipe connection to a hot water storage cylinder is made

- ○ a on the top of the cylinder
- ○ b in the middle of the cylinder
- ○ c in the top third of the cylinder
- ○ d near to the base of the cylinder.

20 Under the Building Regulations, the valve shown below should be fitted to the hot water supply to which sanitary appliance in a new-build dwelling?

- ○ a Kitchen sink
- ○ b Wash hand basin
- ○ c Bath
- ○ d Bidet.

21 Hot water pipework must be insulated when sited in which one of the following locations?

- ○ a On a bathroom wall
- ○ b On a kitchen wall
- ○ c In a garage
- ○ d Run through first-floor timber joists.

22 Which one of the following is the most suitable action to take when a screwdriver-operated spherical plug valve will not isolate the hot water supply to a sanitary appliance?

- ○ a Replace the rubber washer
- ○ b Replace the complete valve
- ○ c Replace the valve gate mechanism
- ○ d Replace the fibre washer.

23 The temperature setting on an overheat thermostat in an immersion heater

- ○ a should be set to operate at 40°C
- ○ b should be set to operate at 60°C
- ○ c is preset by the manufacturer
- ○ d is variable and set by the installer.

24 The warning pipe continually drips from a feed and expansion cistern, and a check on the installation confirms that the float-operated valve is working correctly. Which one of the following could be the cause of the problem?

○ a The service valve to the cistern is defective
○ b The cold-feed pipe has become blocked
○ c The water level is incorrectly set in the cistern
○ d The open-vent pipe has become blocked.

25 When the hot water supply in a rented property is to be turned off to carry out repairs, who should be advised before isolating the supply?

○ a The tenant
○ b The Local Authority
○ c The property owner
○ d The water undertaker.

26 In order to re-washer a hot water tap fed by a combination gas boiler, the best point to isolate the supply causing the least disruption to the customer is

○ a the cold water service valve to the water closet
○ b the cold water service valve to the combination boiler
○ c the cold water supply stop valve
○ d the cold water service valve on the feed and expansion cistern.

27 The Water Regulations identify that when a sanitary appliance is to be permanently removed from the hot water supply

○ a its connecting pipework should be capped at the appliance
○ b the branch to the appliance should be disconnected and capped at its source
○ c its connecting pipework should be disconnected near the appliance
○ d the pipework should be fitted with a service valve and the end capped.

28 Which one of the following should be carried out during commissioning of a hot water system, prior to filling it with water? Completion of

- a   a visual inspection
- b   a soundness test
- c   a performance test
- d   a commissioning record.

29 A hot water system in a single-family dwelling should be flushed with

- a   air
- b   nitrogen
- c   wholesome water
- d   disinfectant fluid.

30 During work on an open-vented hot water system, the installer identifies that the system does not contain an open-vent pipe. Which one of the following actions should be taken?

- a   Isolation of the heat source to the cylinder
- b   Installation of a temperature-relief valve
- c   Installation of a pressure-reducing valve
- d   Isolation of the cold-feed gate valve to the cylinder.

Notes

Notes

Questions and answers

The questions for this unit are repeated below with worked-through answers, which where relevant are linked to an appropriate normative reference source.

Knowledge learning outcome 1
Know the types of hot water system and their layout requirements

1   What type of hot water system is shown in the following diagram?

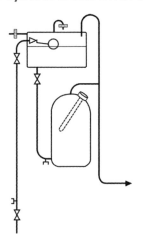

○ a   Single-feed indirect system
○ b   Double-feed indirect system
◉ c   Direct system
○ d   Point of use system.

Answer c
The storage cylinder in the diagram has no primary circuit or heat exchanger, which means it is not indirectly heated (options a and b). It is a centralised storage system rather than point of use (option d). The cylinder is directly heated from an immersion heater (option c).

Notes

2   The lever-operated spherical plug valve shown below uses which one of the following to isolate the water supply?

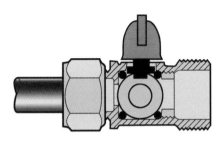

- ○ a   Rubber washer
- ○ b   Ceramic disc
- ◉ c   Rotating ball
- ○ d   Gate-shaped wedge.

Answer c
Rubber washers and ceramic discs (options a and b) are used in taps only, and wedge-shaped gates are the key component in a fullway gate valve (option d). Spherical plug valves use a rotating ball, which has an opening machined in the centre to allow the supply to be isolated when rotated through 90°.

3   What is the minimum size of an open-vent pipe from a direct hot water storage system?

- ○ a   28 mm
- ◉ b   22 mm
- ○ c   15 mm
- ○ d   10 mm.

Answer b
Section 5.3.9.2 of BS 6700 states that the internal bore of any open-vent pipe should not be less than 19 mm, which is the internal bore diameter of 22 mm pipework (option b).

4   **The expanded water from an indirect open-vented hot water system should travel through which pipe to the feed and expansion cistern?**

○ a   Primary open vent
◉ b   Primary cold feed
○ c   Secondary open vent
○ d   Secondary cold feed.

Answer b
The primary water and secondary water in a hot water system are completely separate. The secondary system is fed from the cold water storage cistern to the cylinder. The open vent for the expanded water from the secondary system terminates above the cold water storage cistern, making options c and d incorrect. Expanded water from the primary system travels through the primary cold feed pipe to the feed and expansion cistern (option b); there is minimal movement of expanded water in the open vent pipe, making option a incorrect.

5   **What is the minimum recommended distance that the base to a feed and expansion cistern should project past the edges of the cistern itself?**

○ a   50 mm
○ b   100 mm
◉ c   150 mm
○ d   250 mm.

Answer c
The Building Regulations Approved Document G, Section 3.15 requires that the platform that the cistern rests upon should extend 150 mm beyond the edge of the maximum dimensions of the cistern.

6   **In comparison to a standard indirect cylinder, a super-duty indirect hot water storage cylinder features a**

○ a   higher water capacity
○ b   lower water capacity
◉ c   faster heat recovery rate
○ d   lower heat recovery rate.

Answer c

A super-duty cylinder incorporates a heat exchanger, which has a much larger surface area than a standard indirect cylinder heat exchanger. This allows the heat from the primary circuit to transfer at a faster rate to the secondary circuit water, giving a faster heat recovery rate to the stored water.

7 **A multipoint instantaneous water heater is most suited to providing hot water to**

- ○ a an electric shower
- ⦿ b the outlets in a property with one bathroom
- ○ c the outlets in a property with two bathrooms
- ○ d the outlets in a property with three bathrooms.

Answer b

The flow rate from a multipoint water heater for a small domestic property only normally allows for the appliances in one bathroom to be supplied with water heated to 50°C. For example, a gas multipoint water heater with a flow rate of 12 litres per minute (0.2l/s), gives the minimum flow rate for a bath tap outlet. It would not cope with the demands of multiple bathrooms operating simultaneously, but would cope with the demands of a single bathroom. A point of use instantaneous heater would be used for a single outlet, so option a can be discounted.

8 **The hot water outlet from a multipoint water heater serving a small domestic property is usually sized at**

- ○ a 10 mm
- ⦿ b 15 mm
- ○ c 22 mm
- ○ d 28 mm.

Answer b

The normal outlet size for a multipoint water heater is the same as the input pipework, which for a small-scale multipoint water heater is 15 mm.

9 **In addition to a control thermostat, a new immersion heater must include which one of the following?**

○ a   A temperature-relief valve
◉ b   An overheat thermostat
○ c   A pressure-relief valve
○ d   A double check valve.

Answer b
The Building Regulations Approved Document G, Section 3 states that any direct heat source must have a safety control beyond that of a normal thermostat, this being in the form of a second 'overheat' thermostat which has to be non-self-resetting.

10 **Backflow is most likely to occur in a hot water system when**

◉ a   a tap outlet discharges below the spillover level of a sanitary appliance
○ b   a tap outlet discharges above the spillover level of a sanitary appliance
○ c   the water pressure in the hot water system is too great
○ d   the water flow rate in the hot water system is too great.

Answer a
Backflow normally occurs if the outlet experiences negative pressure, which discounts options c and d. It then has the ability to come into contact with water at its outlet, which leads to option a, as the outlet is below the appliance spillover level. This allows the outlet to come into contact with the appliance's water. With option b it is possible for the water under suction pressure at the tap outlet to jump across the air gap, but this must be small and the suction pressure must be relatively high, making this option less likely than option a.

11 **A shower mixer valve that operates based on the head of water available between the shower head and base of the storage cistern is known as a**

○ a   pumped shower with single impellor
○ b   pumped shower with twin impellor
◉ c   gravity-fed shower
○ d   mains-fed shower.

Answer c
A shower that uses the head of pressure produced in a cistern-fed arrangement to operate rather than by mechanical means is regarded as running by the force of gravity, and is known as a gravity-fed shower.

Knowledge learning outcome 2
Know the site preparation techniques for hot water systems and components

12 **The Water Regulations state that uninsulated hot water pipework must not be embedded in**

- ◉ a chases in external masonry walls
- ○ b an accessible pipe duct
- ○ c timber stud partition walls
- ○ d an accessible pipe chase.

Answer a
The Water Supply (Water Fittings) Regulations Section 3, G71 clearly indicates that hot water pipework should not be placed in an external wall.

13 **Which one of the following types of valves is suitable for use on the cold feed pipe from a storage cistern to a hot water storage cylinder?**

- ○ a Temperature-relief valve
- ○ b Double check valve
- ○ c Screwdown stop valve
- ◉ d Fullway gate valve.

Answer d
Options a and b are not servicing valves, making them inappropriate. Option c is a service valve that is only suitable for use in high-pressure water systems. Option d, the fullway gate valve, has minimal restriction on the flow of water through the valve and is most suited to a lower-pressure installation such as a hot water supply from a storage cistern.

Notes

14 Which one of the following is normally used to make a watertight seal between a tank connector and a plastic feed and expansion cistern?

- ⦿ a   Plastic washers
- ◯ b   Silicone sealant
- ◯ c   Jointing paste
- ◯ d   Fibre washers.

Answer a

When fitting a tank connector it is industry standard practice to use plastic washers, normally made from nylon or other flexible water-repelling plastic to give a tight, rigid seal. Silicone sealant (option b) and fibre washers (option d) are not the types of sealant used for a cistern. Jointing paste (option c) contains oils that can degrade the plastic material.

Knowledge learning outcome 3
Know the installation requirements of hot water systems and components

15 The water flow rate from outlets in a hot water system can be measured using which one of the following?

- ◯ a   Pressure gauge
- ⦿ b   Weir gauge or flow cup
- ◯ c   Multi-meter
- ◯ d   Hygrometer.

Answer b

Option a is a device designed to measure pressure, not flow rate. Option b is an electrical testing device, while a hygrometer (option d) is a device used to measure relative humidity. A weir gauge or flow cup (option b) is used to measure outlet flow rates.

16 Which of the following is true when routing polybutylene pipe through timber first floor joists?

- ⦿ a   Sufficient space must be provided for thermal movement
- ○ b   The pipework must be insulated to guard against fire
- ○ c   The pipework sections must be connected to the electrical earth
- ○ d   Barrier pipe must be used to guard against acid attack from the joists.

Answer a

The nature of plastics is that they expand and contract by far greater amounts when compared with the same size/diameter of metallic pipework, so when installing plastic pipework systems you need to ensure that enough consideration is given to the thermal movement of the pipework. This applies especially when the temperature variation can be quite large, as in hot water systems.

17 An uninsulated 22 mm hot water pipe (dead leg) from a hot water cylinder should be no longer than

- ○ a   3 m
- ○ b   6 m
- ○ c   9 m
- ⦿ d   12 m.

Answer d

BS 6700 Section 5.9.3 clearly defines that hot water pipework up to 22 mm in diameter can have a maximum uninsulated length of 12 m from the cylinder. This is to avoid wastage of water being drawn off before the hot water reaches the outlet.

18 The inlet supply to a feed and expansion cistern is controlled by a

- ○ a   double check valve
- ○ b   temperature-relief valve
- ⦿ c   float-operated valve
- ○ d   pressure-reducing valve.

Notes

Answer c

BS 6700 Section 5.2.3.1.8 clearly defines that the inlet supply to a storage cistern should be fitted with a float-operated valve or a device that is no less effective; the devices mentioned in options a, b and d are not methods of controlling the water supply to a cistern.

19 The cold feed pipe connection to a hot water storage cylinder is made

- ○ a   on the top of the cylinder
- ○ b   in the middle of the cylinder
- ○ c   in the top third of the cylinder
- ⦿ d   near to the base of the cylinder.

Answer d

BS 6700 Section 5.3.9.1 clearly defines that the cold feed to a storage vessel from a cistern should connect near to the base of the vessel and not supply any other fitting.

20 Under the Building Regulations, the valve shown below should be fitted to the hot water supply to which sanitary appliance in a new-build dwelling?

- ○ a   Kitchen sink
- ○ b   Wash hand basin
- ⦿ c   Bath
- ○ d   Bidet.

Answer c
The Building Regulations Approved Document G, Section 3.65 states that any bath installed in a new dwelling must have a thermostatic mixing valve (like the one pictured) fitted and its maximum temperature set to 48°C to prevent scalding. The bath is the only appliance that the occupant could climb into.

21 **Hot water pipework must be insulated when sited in which one of the following locations?**

- ○ a   On a bathroom wall
- ○ b   On a kitchen wall
- ◉ c   In a garage
- ○ d   Run through first-floor timber joists.

Answer c
The Water Supply (Water Fittings) Regulations guidance document (G19.2) recommends that in any situation where hot water pipework passes out of the thermal envelope of the building the pipework should be insulated against the effects of frost; a garage (option c) is such an example.

Knowledge learning outcome 4
Know the service and maintenance requirements of hot water systems and components

22 **Which one of the following is the most suitable action to take when a screwdriver-operated spherical plug valve will not isolate the hot water supply to a sanitary appliance?**

- ○ a   Replace the rubber washer
- ◉ b   Replace the complete valve
- ○ c   Replace the valve gate mechanism
- ○ d   Replace the fibre washer.

Answer b
A screwdriver-operated spherical plug valve is a factory-sealed valve, with no interchangeable parts; therefore the whole valve must be replaced should it become faulty.

23 The temperature setting on an overheat thermostat in an immersion heater

○ a   should be set to operate at 40°C
○ b   should be set to operate at 60°C
◉ c   is preset by the manufacturer
○ d   is variable and set by the installer.

Answer c

Overheat thermostats that are built into all new immersion heaters are preset by the manufacturer to prevent the cylinder from boiling and cannot be altered by the installer.

24 The warning pipe continually drips from a feed and expansion cistern, and a check on the installation confirms that the float-operated valve is working correctly. Which one of the following could be the cause of the problem?

○ a   The service valve to the cistern is defective
○ b   The cold-feed pipe has become blocked
◉ c   The water level is incorrectly set in the cistern
○ d   The open-vent pipe has become blocked.

Answer c

When the water level in a feed and expansion cistern is set, if no allowance is made for the expansion of the water when the heating system is active then the water will expand and possibly overfill the feed and expansion cistern. This is more common on larger systems. A cycle will start which will pass water out of the warning pipe of the cistern when the primary water becomes heated every time the system operates. To fix the problem, the water level must be adjusted to a lower level or the size of the cistern increased.

Knowledge learning outcome 5
Know the decommissioning requirements of hot water systems and components

25 When the hot water supply in a rented property is to be turned off to carry out repairs, who should be advised before isolating the supply?

- ⦿ a The tenant
- ○ b The Local Authority
- ○ c The property owner
- ○ d The water undertaker.

Answer a
The person directly affected by the temporary decommissioning of the system should be the person advised before the supply is terminated.

26 In order to re-washer a hot water tap fed by a combination gas boiler, the best point to isolate the supply causing the least disruption to the customer is

- ○ a the cold water service valve to the water closet
- ⦿ b the cold water service valve to the combination boiler
- ○ c the cold water supply stop valve
- ○ d the cold water service valve on the feed and expansion cistern.

Answer b
When isolating the hot water supply from an instantaneous heating appliance it is possible to isolate the whole property at the stop valve (option c) but this would cause major disruption, so the best option would be to isolate the cold water inlet to the heating appliance (option b) as this would allow the cold water services in the property to operate but temporarily decommission the hot water system.

Notes

27 The Water Regulations identify that when a sanitary appliance is to be permanently removed from the hot water supply

○ a   its connecting pipework should be capped at the appliance

◉ b   the branch to the appliance should be disconnected and capped at its source

○ c   its connecting pipework should be disconnected near the appliance

○ d   the pipework should be fitted with a service valve and the end capped.

Answer b

The Water Supply (Water Fittings) Regulations guidance document (G11.7) identifies that redundant pipework and fittings should have the branch pipe that serviced the fitting isolated and capped off at the source point (option b), rather than just the exposed branches being removed and capped off.

Knowledge learning outcome 6
Know the inspection and soundness testing requirements of hot water systems and components

28 Which one of the following should be carried out during commissioning of a hot water system, prior to filling it with water? Completion of

◉ a   a visual inspection

○ b   a soundness test

○ c   a performance test

○ d   a commissioning record.

Answer a

Option a is the correct answer because of the order for soundness-testing a cold water system, as below:

1) Visual inspection of the system
2) Fill the system with water and check for leaks
3) Soundness-test the system at 150% working pressure for 60 minutes
4) Flush the system with wholesome water.

29 A hot water system in a single-family dwelling should be flushed with

○ a   air
○ b   nitrogen
◉ c   wholesome water
○ d   disinfectant fluid.

Answer c
BS 6700 Section 6.1.10.1 clearly states that all hot and cold water systems should be thoroughly flushed with wholesome water before being put into use.

30 During work on an open-vented hot water system, the installer identifies that the system does not contain an open-vent pipe. Which one of the following actions should be taken?

◉ a   Isolation of the heat source to the cylinder
○ b   Installation of a temperature-relief valve
○ c   Installation of a pressure-reducing valve
○ d   Isolation of the cold-feed gate valve to the cylinder.

Answer a
There would be a serious safety issue with a hot water cylinder that has no means of venting excess pressure. Therefore, until a method of controlling the expansion of water in the system is installed there is only one method to guarantee safety of the system. That is, the removal of all heat sources that could act on the cylinder (option a) would completely remove the risks of a catastrophic failure of the system.

Notes

Notes

Answer key

Sample test 6189-007

Question	Answer	Question	Answer
1	c	16	a
2	c	17	d
3	b	18	c
4	b	19	d
5	c	20	c
6	c	21	c
7	b	22	b
8	b	23	c
9	b	24	c
10	a	25	a
11	c	26	b
12	a	27	b
13	d	28	a
14	a	29	c
15	b	30	a

Understand and apply domestic central heating system installation and maintenance techniques (6189-008)

6189-008

Notes

Sample test

The sample test below is for paper 6189-008, Understand and apply domestic central heating system installation and maintenance techniques. The sample test has 30 questions – remember that the actual exam has 60 questions. The test appears first without answers, so you can use it as a mock exam. It is then repeated with answers and explanations. Finally, there is an answer key for easy reference.

Answer the questions by filling in the circle next to your chosen option.

1   Selective space heating in a dwelling can be described as the heating of

○ a   all rooms to a comfortable design temperature
○ b   all rooms to a low background temperature
○ c   one room to a comfortable design temperature
○ d   some rooms in a dwelling as needed by the occupier.

2   What type of heating system is shown in the following diagram?

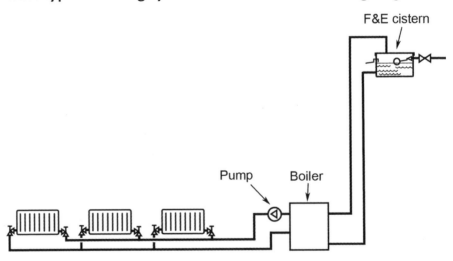

○ a   Gravity heating with mid-position valve
○ b   Pumped heating with 2x two-port valves
○ c   Pumped heating only
○ d   Gravity heating only.

3 **What type of heating system is shown in the following diagram?**

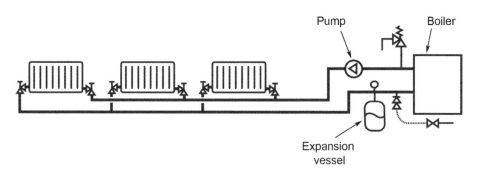

Pump   Boiler

Expansion
vessel

- ○ a   Open-vented heating-only system
- ○ b   Sealed heating-only system
- ○ c   Open-vented fully pumped system
- ○ d   Sealed semi-gravity system.

4 **Which one of the following will be included in an open-vented heating system?**

- ○ a   Pressure-reducing valve
- ○ b   Expansion vessel
- ○ c   Filling loop
- ○ d   Feed and expansion cistern.

5 **Which one of the following components can be used in a mini-bore heating system to distribute circulated water through the main primary flow and return pipework from a central point to individual radiators?**

- ○ a   Hopper head
- ○ b   Distributor head
- ○ c   Manifold
- ○ d   Injector tee.

6 **A solid-fuel heating appliance in which combustion takes place in an enclosed glass-fronted chamber is called**

- ○ a   an open fire
- ○ b   a room heater
- ○ c   an independent boiler
- ○ d   a cooker.

7 **The oil in a pressure-jet burner is forced through which one of the following components during the combustion process?**

○ a   A nozzle
○ b   A venturi
○ c   An injector tee
○ d   A jet stream.

8 **Which one of the following describes a type of gas-fired boiler that takes its air for combustion direct from the outside air?**

○ a   Open-flued
○ b   Room-sealed
○ c   Conventional flued
○ d   Back boiler.

9 **What type of heat emitter is shown in the following photograph?**

○ a   Panel radiator
○ b   Column radiator
○ c   Kick-space radiator
○ d   Low surface temperature radiator.

10 Unwanted (reverse) circulation in central heating pipework can be controlled by installing which one of the following?

○ a   A non-return valve
○ b   A room thermostat
○ c   An injector tee
○ d   A pressure-relief valve.

11 Copper pipework in contact with a chase in a concrete block must be

- a   wrapped in fireproof material
- b   fitted with trace-heating tape
- c   protected against corrosion
- d   fitted with a conductivity strip.

12 The main risk of damage to customer property when removing a solid fuel fireback boiler is created by

- a   fire
- b   soot
- c   toxic smell
- d   vibration.

13 Which one of the following can be used to form the open-vent and cold-feed pipe connections to a fully pumped heating system?

- a   Automatic air vent
- b   Air separator
- c   Manifold
- d   Venturi.

14 Which one of the following may need to be fixed to a radiator before mounting it on a wall surface?

- a   Manifold
- b   Manual air vent
- c   Single check valve
- d   Thermostatic mixing valve.

15 Which one of the following is a 'flame-free' copper pipe jointing process?

- a   Solvent weld
- b   Pressfit
- c   Fusion weld
- d   Slipfit.

16 **Which type of device is used to conserve energy when a frost thermostat is fitted to protect an exposed part of a central heating system?**

○ a   Room thermostat
○ b   Cylinder thermostat
○ c   Pipe thermostat
○ d   Boiler thermostat.

17 **The pipework connections to a motorised valve are normally made using**

○ a   capillary-soldered ring joints
○ b   pressfit joints
○ c   pushfit joints
○ d   compression joints.

18 **Which one of the following is normally included in a filling loop to a sealed central heating system?**

○ a   Double check valve
○ b   Single check valve
○ c   Pressure-relief valve
○ d   Automatic air vent.

19 **Which one of the following can be used to avoid the need for draining a central heating system when extending the number of radiators?**

○ a   Hydraulic test kit
○ b   Air separator
○ c   Automatic air vent
○ d   Pipe-freezing kit.

20 **The maximum permissible heat loss from insulation to heating services pipework is documented in**

○ a   the Domestic Building Services Compliance Guide
○ b   Building Regulations Approved Document J (N in NI)
○ c   British Standard 6700
○ d   the Guide to the Water Regulations.

21 Which one of the following could be the cause of inadequate water circulation through a boiler?

- O a   Defective pressure-relief valve
- O b   Defective pressure-reducing valve
- O c   Incorrectly adjusted automatic bypass valve
- O d   Incorrectly adjusted boiler thermostat.

22 The replacement of which one of the following could be used to rectify a fault in a two-port motorised valve?

- O a   Impellor
- O b   Valve piston
- O c   Valve motor
- O d   Sensor.

23 Which one of the following pieces of information is commonly included on a maintenance record for a heating system?

- O a   Water pressure setting
- O b   Open-vent pipe position
- O c   Type of motorised valve
- O d   Schedule of pipe materials.

24 In order to minimise the impact of heat not being available in a property, at what time of year is it considered best to carry out service work?

- O a   Spring
- O b   Summer
- O c   Autumn
- O d   Winter.

25 When draining down a sealed heating system the water supply

- O a   is isolated at the service valve to the F&E cistern
- O b   is isolated at the service valve to the hot water cylinder
- O c   does not require isolation as it is not permanently connected
- O d   needs pressure to be increased in the system.

26 On draining, the water in a central heating system is normally

- ○ a   wholesome
- ○ b   potable
- ○ c   discoloured
- ○ d   reusable.

27 Which one of the following actions needs to be carried out during draining of a central heating system?

- ○ a   Pressurisation of the system
- ○ b   Allow air to enter the system
- ○ c   Charge the system with nitrogen
- ○ d   Fill the system with corrosion inhibitor.

28 Which one of the following should be carried out before soundness testing a central heating system?

- ○ a   Performance test of the installation
- ○ b   Visual inspection of the installation
- ○ c   Balancing of the radiators
- ○ d   Handover to the customer.

29 The soundness test pressure in a sealed heating system is normally achieved by

- ○ a   using a hydraulic test kit
- ○ b   raising pressure via the filling loop
- ○ c   using a hand bellows
- ○ d   raising pressure at the reducing valve.

30 During soundness testing of a heating system a new fullway gate valve 'sticks' in the closed position. What rectifying action should be carried out?

- ○ a   Re-washer the valve
- ○ b   Replace the valve ceramic disc
- ○ c   Re-washer the gate in the valve
- ○ d   Replace the whole valve.

Questions and answers

The questions for this unit are repeated below with worked-through answers, which where relevant are linked to an appropriate normative reference source.

Notes

Knowledge learning outcome 1
Know the uses of central heating systems in dwellings

1   **Selective space heating in a dwelling can be described as the heating of**

○ a   all rooms to a comfortable design temperature
○ b   all rooms to a low background temperature
○ c   one room to a comfortable design temperature
◉ d   some rooms in a dwelling as needed by the occupier.

Answer d
The types of central heating system are:

Full heating	Heats all rooms to a comfortable design temperature.
Background heating	Heats all rooms to a low background temperature.
Selective heating	Heats some rooms in a dwelling as selected/chosen by the occupier.

Notes

Knowledge learning outcome 2
Know the types of central heating system and their layout requirements

2 **What type of heating system is shown in the following diagram?**

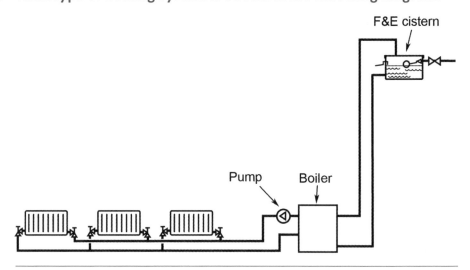

- ○ a   Gravity heating with mid-position valve
- ○ b   Pumped heating with 2x two-port valves
- ◉ c   Pumped heating only
- ○ d   Gravity heating only.

Answer c
The system pictured is not operated by gravity circulation (option d), and it does not show either 2x two-port valves (option b) or a mid-position valve (option a), but does have pumped circulation to a space heating-only system (option c).

Notes

3 **What type of heating system is shown in the following diagram?**

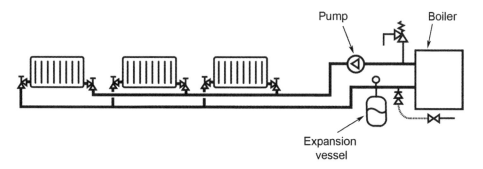

Pump   Boiler

Expansion
vessel

- O a   Open-vented heating-only system
- ⦿ b   Sealed heating-only system
- O c   Open-vented fully pumped system
- O d   Sealed semi-gravity system.

Answer b

The type of system pictured has no feed and expansion cistern,
which removes the possibility of it being open-vented (options a and c).
The system is fully pumped with no hot water circuit so discounting the
sealed semi-gravity system (option d), and confirming that it is a sealed
system serving heating-only (option b).

4 **Which one of the following will be included in an open-vented
heating system?**

- O a   Pressure-reducing valve
- O b   Expansion vessel
- O c   Filling loop
- ⦿ d   Feed and expansion cistern.

Answer d

A sealed central heating system contains a filling loop (option c) and an
expansion vessel (option b). Neither a sealed nor open-vented heating
system contains a pressure-reducing valve (option a). Open-vented
heating systems always contain a feed and expansion cistern (option d).

Notes

5   **Which one of the following components can be used in a mini-bore heating system to distribute circulated water through the main primary flow and return pipework from a central point to individual radiators?**

    ○   a   Hopper head
    ○   b   Distributor head
    ◉   c   Manifold
    ○   d   Injector tee.

Answer c

Often mini-bore heating systems use a purpose-made manifold to evenly distribute the heating water from a central point. This saves time during installation and helps to equalise the flow rates to the system radiators. Option a is a rainwater component, option b is not a recognised plumbing component and option d is used on gravity heating and would not be used on a mini-bore heating system.

6   **A solid-fuel heating appliance in which combustion takes place in an enclosed glass-fronted chamber is called**

    ○   a   an open fire
    ◉   b   a room heater
    ○   c   an independent boiler
    ○   d   a cooker.

Answer b

The combustion in an open fire (option a) takes place in an open, not enclosed, space. With the remaining options, combustion takes place in an enclosed chamber; the room heater (option b) is normally glass-fronted for decorative purposes. With options c and d, the combustion space is not normally visible.

7   **The oil in a pressure-jet burner is forced through which one of the following components during the combustion process?**

    ◉   a   A nozzle
    ○   b   A venturi
    ○   c   An injector tee
    ○   d   A jet stream.

Answer a

Oil-fired pressure-jet appliances function by drawing oil (kerosene) via a pump into the burner assembly, forcing it to atomise and turning the oil into very fine droplets by the use of a nozzle. This atomised mix is then ignited and the heat is used for heating. A venturi is found on gas appliances (option b), an injector tee is a component in a gravity heating system (option c), and a jet stream is not connected with any plumbing systems.

8 **Which one of the following describes a type of gas-fired boiler that takes its air for combustion directly from the outside air?**

- ○ a   Open-flued
- ◉ b   Room-sealed
- ○ c   Conventional flued
- ○ d   Back boiler.

Answer b

Room-sealed or balanced-flued appliances draw the air for the combustion of the fuel directly from the outside air and return the products of combustion directly to the outside air. The remaining descriptions do not cover this method of flue operation.

9 **What type of heat emitter is shown in the following photograph?**

- ○ a   Panel radiator
- ◉ b   Column radiator
- ○ c   Kick-space radiator
- ○ d   Low surface temperature radiator.

Notes

Answer b
The design of this radiator features columns set in rows with air flow spacing between them giving this type of heat emitter its name.

10 Unwanted (reverse) circulation in central heating pipework can be controlled by installing which one of the following?

- ◉ a   A non-return valve
- ○ b   A room thermostat
- ○ c   An injector tee
- ○ d   A pressure-relief valve.

Answer a
A non-return valve, or check valve (option a), in central heating systems is used to ensure that the circulation only occurs in the correct direction. The other options do not provide this function.

Knowledge learning outcome 3
Know the site preparation techniques for central heating systems and components

11 Copper pipework in contact with a chase in a concrete block must be

- ○ a   wrapped in fireproof material
- ○ b   fitted with trace-heating tape
- ◉ c   protected against corrosion
- ○ d   fitted with a conductivity strip.

Answer c
BS 6700 Section 5.8.2.5 reads: 'pipes and pipe joints enclosed in a purpose-made chase in any external wall or located under a suspended floor at ground level or enclosed within a purpose-made sleeve or duct under any solid floor shall, where necessary, be protected from freezing, corrosion and thermal movement.'

As the question does not specify that this is an external wall and could be in a warm area of the building, only the corrosion (option c) and thermal movement aspects apply

12 **The main risk of damage to customer property when removing a solid fuel fireback boiler is created by**

○ a   fire
◉ b   soot
○ c   toxic smell
○ d   vibration.

Answer b

The greatest risk of damage to the customer's property is the spent fuel solids left over by the appliance when it was in operation in the form of carbon powder soot deposits (option b) that will lie in the flue connection to the solid fuel appliance.

13 **Which one of the following can be used to form the open-vent and cold-feed pipe connections to a fully pumped heating system?**

○ a   Automatic air vent
◉ b   Air separator
○ c   Manifold
○ d   Venturi.

Answer b

Air separators can be used to make 'close-coupled' connections of the cold-feed and vent pipes of an open-vented central heating system, in a single pre-fabricated fitting.

Knowledge learning outcome 4

Know the installation requirements of central heating systems and components

14 **Which one of the following may need to be fixed to a radiator before mounting it on a wall surface?**

○ a   Manifold
◉ b   Manual air vent
○ c   Single check valve
○ d   Thermostatic mixing valve.

Answer b

A large proportion of panel radiators require dressing before being mounted on the wall for the pipework connections. This dressing requires the fitting of two control valves, one lockshield and one thermostat radiator valve (TRV), a blank plug and a manual air-bleed vent (option b).

15 Which one of the following is a 'flame-free' copper pipe jointing process?

- ○ a   Solvent weld
- ⦿ b   Pressfit
- ○ c   Fusion weld
- ○ d   Slipfit.

Answer b

The jointing methods in the question are used to joint different pipework materials. Solvent weld (option a) and fusion weld (option c) are used to joint plastics. Only pressfit (option b) is a recognised jointing method for copper pipework that is flame free.

16 Which type of device is used to conserve energy when a frost thermostat is fitted to protect an exposed part of a central heating system?

- ○ a   Room thermostat
- ○ b   Cylinder thermostat
- ⦿ c   Pipe thermostat
- ○ d   Boiler thermostat.

Answer c

In addition to a frost thermostat, which measures the ambient temperature in a cold section of a central heating system, the fitting of a pipe thermostat (option c) can help reduce the operation time of a boiler required to heat the exposed sections. The system will recognise when the pipes have sufficient heat and shut down the heating, rather than allowing constant operation.

17 The pipework connections to a motorised valve are normally made using

- ○ a   capillary-soldered ring joints
- ○ b   pressfit joints
- ○ c   pushfit joints
- ⦿ d   compression joints.

Answer d

The vast majority of motorised valve bodies for domestic central heating systems come with compression joints for connection to the central heating system pipework.

18 Which one of the following is normally included in a filling loop to a sealed central heating system?

- ⊙ a   Double check valve
- ○ b   Single check valve
- ○ c   Pressure-relief valve
- ○ d   Automatic air vent.

Answer a

The Water Supply (Water Fittings) Regulations Schedule 2 Section 24 states that a suitable backflow protection device must be installed on all temporary filling pipework that connects to a domestic sealed central heating circuit. The only suitable item listed is the double check valve.

19 Which one of the following can be used to avoid the need for draining a central heating system when extending the number of radiators?

- ○ a   Hydraulic test kit
- ○ b   Air separator
- ○ c   Automatic air vent
- ⊙ d   Pipe-freezing kit.

Answer d

A hydraulic test kit (option a) is used only for soundness testing and can perform no other function. An air separator (option b) is used to make cold-feed and open-vent pipe connections to a central heating system. An automatic air vent (option c) vents trapped air from a central heating system and cannot be used to temporarily isolate parts of a central heating system. Pipe-freezing kits (option d) can be used to temporarily decommission a section of central heating pipework to allow work to be carried out downstream.

20 The maximum permissible heat loss from insulation to heating services pipework is documented in

- ⊙ a   the Domestic Building Services Compliance Guide
- ○ b   Building Regulations Approved Document J (N in Northern Ireland)
- ○ c   British Standard 6700
- ○ d   the Guide to the Water Regulations.

Notes

Notes

Answer a

The Domestic Building Services Compliance Guide is a supporting document to Part L of the Building Regulations. The document details the maximum heat that can be lost from pipework when connected to a central heating system.

Knowledge learning outcome 5
Know the service and maintenance requirements of central heating systems and components

21 Which one of the following could be the cause of inadequate water circulation through a boiler?

○ a   Defective pressure-relief valve
○ b   Defective pressure-reducing valve
◉ c   Incorrectly adjusted automatic bypass valve
○ d   Incorrectly adjusted boiler thermostat.

Answer c

A defective pressure-relief valve (option a) would not reduce the flow rate through a boiler. A defective pressure-reducing valve (option b) is not a component normally fitted to a central heating system. An incorrectly adjusted boiler thermostat (option d) would affect overall system temperature but not water flow rate. An incorrectly adjusted automatic bypass valve (option c) could divert water away from the boiler and reduce the flow through the boiler.

22 The replacement of which one of the following could be used to rectify a fault in a two-port motorised valve?

○ a   Impellor
○ b   Valve piston
◉ c   Valve motor
○ d   Sensor

Answer c

Motorised valves do not contain impellors (option a), sensors (option d) or pistons (option b). Two-port motorised valves do contain a motor unit mounted on top of the valve body, which is replaceable.

Notes

23 **Which one of the following pieces of information is commonly included on a maintenance record for a heating system?**

- ⦿ a Water pressure setting
- ○ b Open-vent pipe position
- ○ c Type of motorised valve
- ○ d Schedule of pipe materials.

Answer a

Maintenance records contain information about components and items that need to be checked after installation and commissioning. A schedule of pipe materials (option d) and type of motorised valve (option c) would be part of the system specification documents and would not be checked. The open-vent pipe position (option b) would be static and would not require checking as part of routine maintenance. The water system pressure level (option a) in a sealed system would require checking as it can decrease over time.

Knowledge learning outcome 6

Know the decommissioning requirements of central heating systems and components

24 **In order to minimise the impact of heat not being available in a property, at what time of year is it considered best to carry out service work?**

- ○ a Spring
- ⦿ b Summer
- ○ c Autumn
- ○ d Winter.

Answer b

Conducting maintenance and repairs in the summer months would have the least impact on customers as there is usually less call for heating in those months.

25 **When draining down a sealed heating system the water supply**

- ○ a is isolated at the service valve to the F&E cistern
- ○ b is isolated at the service valve to the hot water cylinder
- ⦿ c does not require isolation as it is not permanently connected
- ○ d needs pressure to be increased in the system.

Answer c

A sealed central heating system to a domestic property does not normally feature a permanent connection to a water supply, as it is filled from a removable filling loop, and therefore does not require isolating from the water supply.

26 On draining, the water in a central heating system is normally

- ○ a   wholesome
- ○ b   potable
- ◉ c   discoloured
- ○ d   reusable

Answer c

Water in central heating systems should contain additives to resist system corrosion, and normally magnetite in suspension making the liquid dark brown or black in colour. Because of the contamination the water is not considered wholesome, drinkable/potable or suitable for use in water recycling systems (grey water).

27 Which one of the following actions needs to be carried out during draining of a central heating system?

- ○ a   Pressurisation of the system
- ◉ b   Allow air to enter the system
- ○ c   Charge the system with nitrogen
- ○ d   Fill the system with corrosion inhibitor.

Answer b

When draining a central heating system, air must be introduced to allow the whole system's contents to be drained, otherwise large parts of the system will not fully drain.

Knowledge learning outcome 7
Know the inspection and soundness testing requirements of central heating systems and components

28 Which one of the following should be carried out before soundness-testing a central heating system?

- ○ a   Performance test of the installation
- ◉ b   Visual inspection of the installation
- ○ c   Balancing of the radiators
- ○ d   Handover to the customer.

Answer b

Option b is the correct answer, as laid down in the procedure for soundness-testing a central heating system as shown below:

1) Visual inspection of the installation
2) Fill the system with water and check for leaks
3) Soundness test the system at 150% working pressure for 60 minutes
4) Flush the system with wholesome water.

29 The soundness test pressure in a sealed heating system is normally achieved by

- ○ a   using a hydraulic test kit
- ◉ b   raising pressure via the filling loop
- ○ c   using a hand bellows
- ○ d   raising pressure at the reducing valve.

Answer b

The test pressure is normally achieved by over-pressurisation from the mains supply at the filling loop (option b). It is possible to use a hydraulic test kit (option a) but this would not be deemed necessary in the majority of cases where a high water mains pressure is available.

30 During soundness-testing of a heating system a new fullway gate valve 'sticks' in the closed position. What rectifying action should be carried out?

- ○ a   Re-washer the valve
- ○ b   Replace the valve ceramic disc
- ○ c   Re-washer the gate in the valve
- ◉ d   Replace the whole valve.

Answer d

There is no option but to replace gate valves when they become defective by the gate itself becoming wedged in position (option d) as the valve internal mechanism does not normally contain serviceable parts.

Answer key

Sample test 6189-008

Question	Answer	Question	Answer
1	d	16	c
2	c	17	d
3	b	18	a
4	d	19	d
5	c	20	a
6	b	21	c
7	a	22	c
8	b	23	a
9	b	24	b
10	a	25	c
11	c	26	c
12	b	27	b
13	b	28	b
14	b	29	b
15	b	30	d

Understand and apply domestic rainwater system installation and maintenance techniques (6189-009)

6189-009

Sample test

The sample test below is for paper 6189-009, Understand and apply domestic rainwater system installation and maintenance techniques. The sample test has 30 questions – remember that the actual exam has 35 questions. The test appears first without answers, so you can use it as a mock exam. It is then repeated with answers and explanations. Finally, there is an answer key for easy reference.

Answer the questions by filling in the circle next to your chosen option.

1 One of the main purposes of a gravity rainwater system attached to a building is to

- ○ a   prevent corrosion of the building
- ○ b   protect the foundations of the building
- ○ c   reduce humidity levels in buildings
- ○ d   provide purified water for use in buildings.

2 Which one of the following is a traditional guttering material that was historically used on older properties, eg Victorian?

- ○ a   Cast iron
- ○ b   Low-carbon steel
- ○ c   Polybutylene
- ○ d   Magnesium.

3   What type of gutter is shown in the following photograph?

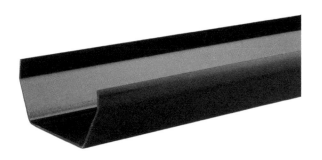

○ a   Ogee section
○ b   Tapered section
○ c   Half-round section
○ d   Square section.

4   **The fitting shown in the photograph is used with which type of rainwater pipe?**

○ a   Half-round section
○ b   Oval section
○ c   Ogee section
○ d   Round section.

5   When identifying the size of gutters required for a domestic property, which one of the following needs to be taken into consideration?

○ a   The capacity of the water main
○ b   The quantity of gutter brackets to be used
○ c   The roof area of the building
○ d   The coefficient of linear expansion of the materials.

6   Which one of the following is normally used as a jointing material in PVC-u gutter fittings?

○ a   Silicone sealant
○ b   Rubber sealing strip
○ c   Fibre rope sealing strip
○ d   Putty and paint.

7   Which one of the following is normally used as a sealant material when jointing PVC-u rainwater pipes?

○ a   Silicone sealant
○ b   Solvent weld cement
○ c   Putty and paint
○ d   Rubber sealing strip.

8   Which one of the following fittings is used to joint two pieces of gutter together on a straight run?

○ a   Stop end
○ b   Union
○ c   Angle
○ d   Running outlet.

9   Which one of the following fittings is used to joint pieces of gutter around a bay window?

○ a   Angle
○ b   Union
○ c   Running outlet
○ d   Stop end.

10 **What type of gutter bracket is normally used where the gutter is to be fixed to a timber board?**

○ a   Drive-in bracket
○ b   Fascia bracket
○ c   Rafter bracket
○ d   Soffit bracket.

11 **Which one of the following rainwater pipe components can be used to collect water from two rainwater pipes and discharge it into a single pipe?**

○ a   Hopper head
○ b   Shoe
○ c   Running outlet
○ d   Offset.

12 **What is the name of the rainwater pipe component shown in the image?**

○ a   Union connector
○ b   Shoe
○ c   Offset
○ d   Angle.

13 **Which one of the following is used to identify the capacity of a gutter system?**

○ a   Building Regulations Approved Document
○ b   BS EN 12056
○ c   BS EN 12983
○ d   Manufacturer catalogues.

14 When replacing gutters that are fixed to timber boards on an existing building, which one of the following actions should be considered?

- O a Repainting of the timber boards before new gutter installation
- O b Repainting of the timber boards after new gutter installation
- O c Application of electrolytic coating to the PVC-u gutter
- O d Installation of a lightning conductor to the PVC-u gutter.

15 Fascia brackets are normally secured to timber surfaces using

- O a slotted head steel screws
- O b stainless steel or brass screws
- O c copper clout nails
- O d coach bolts.

16 PVC-u rainwater pipe is normally cut with a

- O a pad saw
- O b hole saw
- O c hack saw
- O d mitre saw.

17 By how much would a 6 m length of PVC-u gutter increase in length when heated by sunlight from 10°C to 35°C?

The coefficient of linear expansion of PVC-u is 0.06 mm/m/°C
- O a 5 mm
- O b 9 mm
- O c 15 mm
- O d 22 mm.

18 What is the minimum fall across a length of PVC-u gutter?

- O a No fall
- O b 1 in 600
- O c 1 in 900
- O d 1 in 1200.

19 What is the vertical drop across a 9 m length of gutter if it is laid to a fall of 1 in 600?

○ a   10 mm
○ b   15 mm
○ c   20 mm
○ d   25 mm.

20 A length of gutter is secured to a PVC-u fascia bracket by a

○ a   screw fastening
○ b   bolt fastening
○ c   clip-in fastening
○ d   rubber fastening.

21 What is the recommended bracket spacing interval for a 68 mm vertically fixed rainwater pipe?

○ a   0.6 m
○ b   1.2 m
○ c   1.5 m
○ d   2.0 m.

22 What type of below-ground drainage system is indicated by a rainwater pipe connection using a 90° bend direct to a drain?

○ a   Surface water-only system
○ b   Cesspool-only system
○ c   Foul-water system
○ d   Combined waste-water system.

23 What type of rainwater pipe component is normally used to discharge water over a gulley grid?

○ a   Union connector
○ b   Hopper head
○ c   Angle
○ d   Shoe.

Notes

24 The maximum distance between an unsupported gutter fitting, eg an angle and the nearest gutter bracket is

- ○ a 50 mm
- ○ b 100 mm
- ○ c 150 mm
- ○ d 250 mm.

25 Which one of the following would normally form part of a periodic maintenance programme carried out on a PVC-u gutter system?

- ○ a Clear the gutter of any potential blockages
- ○ b Replacement of all rubber seals
- ○ c Replacement of glued gutter seals
- ○ d Check for mains water contamination.

26 Water running over the front face of a gutter connected to a rainwater pipe that is full of water would indicate a blockage in which one of the following?

- ○ a The top of the rainwater pipe
- ○ b The gutter running outlet
- ○ c The gutter union connector
- ○ d The surface water drain.

27 Which one of the following is the greatest health risk when handling gutters that are fouled with bird droppings?

- ○ a Smell from the droppings
- ○ b Ingestion of the droppings
- ○ c Slipping on the droppings
- ○ d Toxic shock from the droppings.

28 Which one of the following could form part of the visual inspection of a rainwater system carried out during soundness testing?

- ○ a PVC-u vertical rainwater pipe brackets positioned at 3.5 m intervals
- ○ b PVC-u gutter fittings fully jointed with silicone-type sealant
- ○ c Check for the installation of traps at running outlets
- ○ d Check for correct expansion space in fittings.

29 A soundness test on a gravity rainwater system can be carried out by

○ a   introducing compressed air to the system at 35 psi pressure
○ b   spraying water on the roof of the building with a hosepipe
○ c   pressurising the system to 1.5 times its working pressure
○ d   pressurising the system to 1.0 bar pressure.

30 Which one of the following is likely to be the cause of a PVC-u gutter system that is 'bowing' (distorting) between the brackets?

○ a   Failure of the bracket fixings
○ b   Ultraviolet breakdown of the PVC-u material
○ c   Failure of the gutter seals
○ d   Insufficient room for thermal movement.

Questions and answers

The questions for this unit are repeated below with worked-through answers, which where relevant are linked to an appropriate normative reference source.

Knowledge learning outcome 1
Know the general principles of gravity rainwater systems

1 **One of the main purposes of a gravity rainwater system attached to a building is to**

○ a   prevent corrosion of the building
◉ b   protect the foundations of the building
○ c   reduce humidity levels in buildings
○ d   provide purified water for use in buildings.

Answer b
One of the main aims of a rainwater system is to prevent accumulation of water in the foundations, which could lead to damage to those foundations (option b). Options c and d are not functions of a rainwater system whereas with option a, the building materials should naturally be corrosion free with no link to the rainwater system.

2 **Which one of the following is a traditional guttering material that was historically used on older properties, eg Victorian?**

◉ a   Cast iron
○ b   Low-carbon steel
○ c   Polybutylene
○ d   Magnesium.

Answer a
Historically, cast iron was used as a guttering material because it was a cheap, strong material; it is not however widely installed any more. This is because it requires constant maintenance (ie painting) to prevent corrosion, unlike plastic systems. To repair or replace leaking joints or cracked sections of gutter on cast-iron systems also takes much longer than the plastic equivalents.

Notes

3 **What type of gutter is shown in the photograph?**

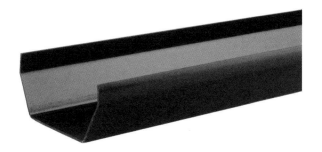

○ a   Ogee section
○ b   Tapered section
○ c   Half-round section
◉ d   Square section.

Answer d
The type of gutter pictured is known as square-section guttering, as
it is the only plastic guttering type with rigid sharp angles; all the other
types have a rounded or arched profile.

4 **The fitting shown in the photograph is used with which type
of rainwater pipe?**

○ a   Half-round section
○ b   Oval section
○ c   Ogee section
◉ d   Round section.

Notes

Answer d

There are only two types of downpipe used; square section and round section. The fitting in the picture clearly shows a round-section socket connection.

Knowledge learning outcome 2
Know the layout requirements of gravity rainwater systems

5 When identifying the size of gutters required for a domestic property, which one of the following needs to be taken into consideration?

- ○ a   The capacity of the water main
- ○ b   The quantity of gutter brackets to be used
- ⊙ c   The roof area of the building
- ○ d   The coefficient of linear expansion of the materials.

Answer c

The method for this calculation can be found in BS EN 12056 Part 3. To work out the capacity of gutter required to serve a building you use the area of the roof and the average intensity of the rainfall for the region that the building is located.

6 Which one of the following is normally used as a jointing material in PVC-u gutter fittings?

- ○ a   Silicone sealant
- ⊙ b   Rubber sealing strip
- ○ c   Fibre rope sealing strip
- ○ d   Putty and paint.

Answer b

Click-fit gutter fittings use rubber strips to form the watertight seal between the fitting and the guttering. The other options are not used with PVC-u fittings.

7 Which one of the following is normally used as a sealant material when jointing PVC-u rainwater pipes?

- ○ a   Silicone sealant
- ⊙ b   Solvent weld cement
- ○ c   Putty and paint
- ○ d   Rubber sealing strip.

Answer b

When jointing rainwater pipes, solvent cement is normally used to make fixed joints, but care must be taken to allow for thermal movement.

8 **Which one of the following fittings is used to joint two pieces of gutter together on a straight run?**

○ a   Stop end
◉ b   Union
○ c   Angle
○ d   Running outlet.

Answer b

Gutter unions (option b) are used to connect two lengths of gutter together on straight runs. Stop ends (option a) are used to end gutter runs, running outlets (option d) are used to connect gutters to rainwater pipes and gutter angles (option c) are used to change the direction of gutter runs.

9 **Which one of the following fittings is used to joint pieces of gutter around a bay window?**

◉ a   Angle
○ b   Union
○ c   Running outlet
○ d   Stop end.

Answer a

Gutter angles are used to connect two pieces of guttering together, but unlike unions they are designed to adapt guttering to changes in direction. Gutter unions (option b) are used to connect two lengths of gutter together on straight runs. Stop ends (option d) are used to end gutter runs, and running outlets (option c) are used to connect guttering to rainwater pipes.

10 **What type of gutter bracket is normally used where the gutter is to be fixed to a timber board?**

○ a   Drive-in bracket
◉ b   Fascia bracket
○ c   Rafter bracket
○ d   Soffit bracket.

Notes

Answer b

Timber boards are used as a front facing as part of timber roof eaves; this facing or fascia board often has guttering attached to it by the use of 'fascia' brackets.

11 Which one of the following rainwater pipe components can be used to collect water from two rainwater pipes and discharge it into a single pipe?

◉ a   Hopper head
◯ b   Shoe
◯ c   Running outlet
◯ d   Offset.

Answer a

Rainwater hopper heads can be used to collect water from both weir outlets from flat and pitched roofs and also are used to join two downpipes together by having two downpipes discharge into the hopper and one downpipe leaving the hopper outlet.

12 What is the name of the rainwater pipe component shown in the image?

◯ a   Union connector
◯ b   Shoe
◉ c   Offset
◯ d   Angle.

Answer c

Gutter offsets are used to connect eaves guttering to a rainwater pipe via a running outlet or to pass obstacles on the wall surface.

Knowledge learning outcome 3
Know the site preparation techniques for gravity rainwater systems

13 Which one of the following is used to identify the capacity of a gutter system?

- ○ a   Building Regulations Approved Document
- ○ b   BS EN 12056
- ○ c   BS EN 12983
- ◉ d   Manufacturer catalogues.

Answer d
Exact gutter capacities can only be found in manufacturers' literature as each manufacturer will produce guttering with slight variations, which will affect the capacity of the gutter.

14 When replacing gutters that are fixed to timber boards on an existing building, which one of the following actions should be considered?

- ◉ a   Repainting of the timber boards before new gutter installation
- ○ b   Repainting of the timber boards after new gutter installation
- ○ c   Application of electrolytic coating to the PVC-u gutter
- ○ d   Installation of a lightning conductor to the PVC-u gutter.

Answer a
While the guttering is being replaced there will be the opportunity to carry out maintenance or repairs on the timber fascia boards, eg painting, which will prolong its lifespan.

15 Fascia brackets are normally secured to timber surfaces using

- ○ a   slotted head steel screws
- ◉ b   stainless steel or brass screws
- ○ c   copper clout nails
- ○ d   coach bolts.

Answer b
Stainless steel or brass screws are the best fixing method for gutter fittings as steel screws, bolts or copper nails will corrode in the damp environment and will make repairs, maintenance and replacements of gutter fittings difficult in the future.

Notes

16 PVC-u rainwater pipe is normally cut with a

○ a   pad saw
○ b   hole saw
◉ c   hack saw
○ d   mitre saw.

Answer c

PVC-u gutter is best cut with a fine-tooth hack saw as it gives the best results. Saw types such as coping or pad saws do not give enough control of the cut, often leaving uneven edges. Coarse-tooth saws such as wood saws are not suitable for cutting plastics and often slip across the surface of the material, which can lead to accidents, making them dangerous to use.

Knowledge learning outcome 4
Know the installation requirements of gravity rainwater systems

17 By how much would a 6 m length of PVC-u gutter increase in length when heated by sunlight from 10°C to 35°C?

The coefficient of linear expansion of PVC-u is 0.06 mm/m/°C.

○ a   5 mm
◉ b   9 mm
○ c   15 mm
○ d   22 mm.

Answer b

The coefficient of linear expansion of PVC-u is 0.06 mm/m/°C; to complete this calculation we must find and fill in the numbers in the equation.

The length of gutter is 6 m. The temperature difference is 35°C minus 10°C or 25°C. When we use these numbers in the equation, we get 0.06 mm x 6 x 25 = 9 mm.

18 What is the minimum fall across a length of PVC-u gutter?

◉ a   No fall
○ b   1 in 600
○ c   1 in 900
○ d   1 in 1200.

Notes

Answer a

BS EN 12056 Section 5.1.1 states that gutters may be laid level or to a gradient, unless stated otherwise by local or national regulation. In England and Wales there is no regulation that insists on a gutter fall, although a fall is recommended.

19 What is the vertical drop across a 9 m length of gutter if it is laid to a fall of 1 in 600?

- ○ a   10 mm
- ◉ b   15 mm
- ○ c   20 mm
- ○ d   25 mm.

Answer b

To calculate the fall you must take the length of gutter run and divide it by 600.

9000 mm ÷ 600 mm = 15 mm fall.

20 A length of gutter is secured to a PVC-u fascia bracket by a

- ○ a   screw fastening
- ○ b   bolt fastening
- ◉ c   clip-in fastening
- ○ d   rubber fastening.

Answer c

Fascia brackets do not use a screw or bolt fastening mechanism to fix the gutter in position because the ability to unfasten guttering without the use of tools is a massive advantage when working in-situ at height. A modern PVC-u guttering system uses a clip-in fastening system.

21 What is the recommended bracket spacing interval for a 68 mm vertically fixed rainwater pipe?

- ○ a   0.6 m
- ○ b   1.2 m
- ○ c   1.5 m
- ◉ d   2.0 m.

Notes

Answer d

The following table outlines the recommended bracket spacing intervals for plastic rainwater pipes.

Rainwater pipe clip centres		
Pipe size	Vertical	Horizontal
55 mm	1.2	0.6
61 mm	2.0	1.0
68 mm	2.0	1.0
70 mm	2.0	1.0
82 mm	2.0	1.0
110 mm	2.0	1.0

22 What type of below-ground drainage system is indicated by a rainwater pipe connection using a 90° bend direct to a drain?

- ⦿ a   Surface water-only system
- ◯ b   Cesspool-only system
- ◯ c   Foul-water system
- ◯ d   Combined waste-water system.

Answer a

Building Regulation Approved Document H Section 1 states that any connection to the drainage system that receives foul water must be made by a trap or other suitable device. Cesspools (option b), foul-water drains (option c) and combined drains (option d) all receive foul water and as such any connections to them must be made via a trap. However, the connection in the above question does not incorporate a trap so the rainwater must be discharging into a system that serves only surface water.

23 What type of rainwater pipe component is normally used to discharge water over a gulley grid?

- ◯ a   Union connector
- ◯ b   Hopper head
- ◯ c   Angle
- ⦿ d   Shoe.

Answer d

The correct method of terminating a rainwater pipe over a gulley grid is via the use of a shoe because this fitting is designed to facilitate the rainwater leaving the rainwater pipe evenly without causing any splashing or spraying. A hopper head (option b) is not used at ground level, a union connector (option a) is used to connect two straight guttering sections together and an angel (option c) is used to divert the guttering around a bay window.

24 **The maximum distance between an unsupported gutter fitting, eg an angle and the nearest gutter bracket is**

- ○ a   50 mm
- ○ b   100 mm
- ◉ c   150 mm
- ○ d   250 mm.

Answer c

In BS EN 12056-3:2000 National Annex NE Section 2.2 it clearly states that the supporting bracket from a union or angle should be 150 mm maximum from the gutter end.

Knowledge learning outcome 5
Know the service and maintenance requirements of gravity rainwater systems

25 **Which one of the following would normally form part of a periodic maintenance programme carried out on a PVC-u gutter system?**

- ◉ a   Clear the gutter of any potential blockages
- ○ b   Replacement of all rubber seals
- ○ c   Replacement of glued gutter seals
- ○ d   Check for mains water contamination.

Answer a

Option d, mains water contamination, is not associated with a rainwater system. Gutter seals are not glued (option c) and replacement of all gutter seals (option b) should not be necessary. This leaves only a check for potential blockages (option a) as an activity that would normally be carried out during a periodic maintenance programme.

26 Water running over the front face of a gutter connected to a rainwater pipe that is full of water would indicate a blockage in which one of the following?

○ a   The top of the rainwater pipe
○ b   The gutter running outlet
○ c   The gutter union connector
◉ d   The surface water drain.

Answer d
If the top of the rainwater pipe was blocked at the top of the pipe (option a) or the running outlet was blocked (option b) the rainwater pipe would not be full of water, as it would drain away. The indication of the whole pipe being full of water is that the drain itself (option d) must have stopped receiving rainwater and is blocked.

27 Which one of the following is the greatest health risk when handling gutters that are fouled with bird droppings?

○ a   Smell from the droppings
◉ b   Ingestion of the droppings
○ c   Slipping on the droppings
○ d   Toxic shock from the droppings.

Answer b
Bird droppings or manure can spread fungal, bacterial, viral and even parasitic diseases that can cause serious illnesses. The droppings may also contain ticks and fleas that the birds carry, which can be a health hazard, making ingestion (option b) the major problem identified.

Knowledge learning outcome 6
Know the inspection and testing requirements of gravity rainwater systems

28 Which one of the following could form part of the visual inspection of a rainwater system carried out during soundness testing?

○ a   PVC-u vertical rainwater pipe brackets positioned at 3.5 m intervals
○ b   PVC-u gutter fittings fully jointed with silicone-type sealant
○ c   Check for the installation of traps at running outlets
◉ d   Check for correct expansion space in fittings.

Answer d
Because of the large amount of thermal movement associated with plastic guttering, there is a need to check that the correct amount of expansion space was left when the guttering was assembled.

29 A soundness test on a gravity rainwater system can be carried out by

○ a   introducing compressed air to the system at 35 psi pressure
◉ b   spraying water on the roof of the building with a hosepipe
○ c   pressurising the system to 1.5 times its working pressure
○ d   pressurising the system to 1.0 bar pressure.

Answer b
There is very little to a soundness test of eaves guttering other than ensuring that it remains watertight under working conditions. The application of a hosepipe to the roof area can simulate the levels of water flow that can occur in working conditions.

30 Which one of the following is likely to be the cause of a PVC-u gutter system that is 'bowing' (distorting) between the brackets?

○ a   Failure of the bracket fixings
○ b   Ultraviolet breakdown of the PVC-u material
○ c   Failure of the gutter seals
◉ d   Insufficient room for thermal movement.

Answer d
If long runs of gutter are fixed into position and no room is left for thermal movement as the gutter heats up it will bend and distort out of shape, and in extreme cases break. Manufacturers recommend only assembling guttering up to the expansion marks in the unions, angles and running outlets to allow for thermal movement of the guttering.

Notes

Notes

Answer key

Sample test 6189-009

Question	Answer	Question	Answer
1	b	16	c
2	a	17	b
3	d	18	a
4	d	19	b
5	c	20	c
6	b	21	d
7	b	22	a
8	b	23	d
9	a	24	c
10	b	25	a
11	a	26	d
12	c	27	b
13	d	28	d
14	a	29	b
15	b	30	d

Understand and apply domestic above-ground drainage system installation and maintenance techniques (6189-010)

6189-010

Sample test

The sample test below is for paper 6189-010, Understand and apply domestic above-ground drainage system installation and maintenance techniques. The sample test has 30 questions – remember that the actual exam has 50 questions. The test appears first without answers, so you can use it as a mock exam. It is then repeated with answers and explanations. Finally, there is an answer key for easy reference.

Answer the questions by filling in the circle next to your chosen option.

1   **What type of wash hand basin is shown in the following photograph?**

○ a   Countertop
○ b   Pedestal
○ c   Hand rinse
○ d   Under countertop.

2   **Where does the overflow normally discharge to in a new WC fitted with a drop-valve mechanism?**

○ a   To the outside air
○ b   To the toilet pan
○ c   To the toilet cistern
○ d   To the basin waste.

3 Which type of sanitary pipework system will normally be used in a two-storey house with all appliances closely grouped around the stack?

- ○ a Primary ventilated stack system
- ○ b Secondary ventilated stack system
- ○ c Ventilated branch discharge system
- ○ d Stub stack system.

4 What type of trap seal loss can occur at the base of a discharge stack due to the positive pressure produced in the stack itself?

- ○ a Self-siphonage
- ○ b Evaporation
- ○ c Induced siphonage
- ○ d Compression.

5 A branch connection should NOT be made into a discharge stack serving a two-storey property within what vertical dimension of the drain invert?

- ○ a 200 mm
- ○ b 350 mm
- ○ c 450 mm
- ○ d 600 mm.

6 What is the minimum size of discharge stack that can be used in a two-storey property?

- ○ a 50 mm
- ○ b 75 mm
- ○ c 100 mm
- ○ d 150 mm.

7 **In the following diagram, the trap seal is shown at dimension**

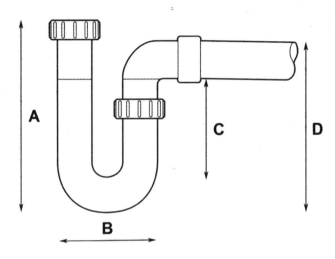

- ○ a A
- ○ b B
- ○ c C
- ○ d D.

8 **Which one of the following is suitable for use when making a branch connection into a discharge stack immediately opposite another branch connection?**

- ○ a A strap boss with swept entry
- ○ b A junction with swept entry
- ○ c A boss pipe with 90° entry
- ○ d A junction with 90° entry.

9 **Why should an air-admittance valve NOT be installed in a very dusty environment?**

- ○ a The rubber diaphragm will perish quickly
- ○ b The filter will be prone to continual blocking
- ○ c The valve will suffer from excessive corrosion
- ○ d The valve will rupture due to excessive pressure.

10 **What trap-seal depth must be used when connecting a kitchen sink directly to a below-ground drainage system?**

○ a   19 mm
○ b   38 mm
○ c   50 mm
○ d   75 mm.

11 **Which British Standard makes recommendations on the activity space that should be provided around sanitary appliances?**

○ a   BS 5440
○ b   BS 6465
○ c   BS EN 12056
○ d   BS EN 12983.

12 **What is the maximum depth of pipe notch that can be cut in a first-floor joist that has a depth of 250 mm?**

○ a   22 mm
○ b   31 mm
○ c   52 mm
○ d   67 mm.

13 **The component in the following photograph is used for connecting**

○ a   two PVC-u pipes together
○ b   a PVC-u pipe to a clay drain
○ c   a PVC-u pipe to a WC pan
○ d   two PVC-u pipes to a bath.

Notes

14 Which one of the following can be used for removing a blockage in a waste pipe?

○ a   An auger
○ b   A gulley grab
○ c   A drain plug
○ d   A siphon.

15 The seal between a close-coupled WC flushing cistern and its pan is made watertight by using

○ a   silicone sealant
○ b   a 'top hat' washer
○ c   a 'doughnut' washer
○ d   putty and paste.

16 Why should a gap be left in a ring-seal joint (as shown in the diagram) between the pipe ends and fitting shoulders?

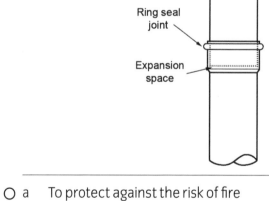

Ring seal joint

Expansion space

○ a   To protect against the risk of fire
○ b   To permit thermal movement
○ c   To permit access for maintenance
○ d   To protect against trap-seal loss.

17 By how much would 10 m of PVC-u pipe expand if it were to be heated from 10°C to 40°C and its coefficient of linear expansion was 0.06 mm/m/°C?

○ a   7 mm
○ b   12 mm
○ c   18 mm
○ d   25 mm.

18 Which one of the following is a suitable fixing for a wash hand basin?

○ a   Steel screw
○ b   Brass screw
○ c   Copper nail
○ d   Steel bolt.

19 A waste appliance can discharge into a

○ a   soakaway
○ b   surface water drain
○ c   foul-water drain
○ d   water main.

20 A branchpipe discharging to a new gulley should terminate

○ a   above the gulley grid
○ b   below the gulley grid
○ c   below the gulley water seal
○ d   through the gulley water seal.

21 When jointing a new waste strap boss to an existing painted PVC-u discharge stack, which one of the following should form part of the jointing process?

○ a   Removal of the paint in the proposed strap boss location
○ b   Repainting of the stack in the proposed strap boss location
○ c   Use of white spirit to make the joint between boss and stack
○ d   Use of linseed oil putty to make the joint between boss and stack.

Notes

22 Which one of the following is the most likely cause of a drop valve constantly discharging water into a WC pan?

○ a   Siphon washer failure
○ b   Service valve failure
○ c   Grit on the drop valve seal
○ d   Blockage of the overflow.

23 A blockage in a waste appliance trap can be removed by using

○ a   drain rods
○ b   a force cup
○ c   a gulley grab
○ d   silicone sealant.

24 Which one of the following is most likely to be included on a record completed during the scheduled maintenance of a sanitation system?

○ a   A check to confirm that all traps have been replaced
○ b   The replacement of 'o' ring seals on all pipework joints
○ c   The application of new glue to all solvent welded joints
○ d   A check to confirm that pipework is correctly supported.

25 When taking sanitary appliances out of use in order to work on them, isolation of which one of the following will cause the greatest disruption to the occupants of dwellings?

○ a   Sinks
○ b   Baths
○ c   Wash hand basins
○ d   WCs.

26 When removing a WC pan connected to an existing sanitary pipework system, which one of the following is considered to be the main nuisance if the pan is to be left disconnected for a significant period of time?

○ a   Noise
○ b   Smells
○ c   Dust production
○ d   Fire risk.

27 Which one of the following will fully prevent a WC from being flushed while work is taking place on a sanitary pipework system?

- a   Isolation of the water supply and emptying of the cistern
- b   Temporary capping of the sanitary pipework with a drain plug
- c   Covering the top of the WC pan with cling film
- d   Use of a warning notice placed on the WC pan.

28 Which one of the following would be included in a visual inspection of a new sanitary appliance system as part of the commissioning process?

- a   Check for overall compliance of the installation with statutory regulations
- b   Check for operation to ensure that trap seals are not lost during operation
- c   Confirmation that all branch pipework includes a ventilating pipe
- d   Confirmation that the system will be disinfected as part of commissioning.

29 During a pressure test on a sanitary pipework system, the pressure in the system is raised using

- a   a hydraulic test kit
- b   hand bellows
- c   a manometer
- d   a foot pump.

30 A leak can be detected on a plastic sanitary pipework system during pressure testing by

- a   using soap solution
- b   using a gas detector
- c   wrapping joints with paper
- d   looking for signs of smoke.

Notes

Questions and answers

The questions for this unit are repeated below with worked-through answers, which where relevant are linked to an appropriate normative reference source.

Knowledge learning outcome 1
Know the uses of sanitary appliances and their operating principles

1   What type of wash hand basin is shown in the following photograph?

○ a   Countertop
○ b   Pedestal
◉ c   Hand rinse
○ d   Under countertop

Answer c
The picture shows a wall-hung basin with a pop-up waste and single tap hole, commonly used for hand washing only. The picture does not feature a pedestal (option b) nor is the basin mounted in a countertop (options a and d).

2   Where does the overflow normally discharge to in a new WC fitted with a drop-valve mechanism?

○ a   To the outside air
◉ b   To the toilet pan
○ c   To the toilet cistern
○ d   To the basin waste.

Answer b
Modern drop-valve WC cisterns have internal overflows included as part of the normal design. This means that when fault conditions occur, the water from the warning pipe empties into the toilet pan.

Notes

Knowledge learning outcome 2
Know the types of sanitary pipework system and their layout requirements

3 **Which type of sanitary pipework system will normally be used in a two-storey house with all appliances closely grouped around the stack?**

◉ a   Primary ventilated stack system
○ b   Secondary ventilated stack system
○ c   Ventilated branch discharge system
○ d   Stub stack system.

Answer a
The primary ventilated stack system is most commonly used in domestic properties because:
– it is economical with materials and installation time
– it is suitable for properties where appliances are closely grouped around the stack, which is the majority of domestic properties
– there are normally minimal pressure fluctuations created within the main stack that would normally require an alternative system.

4 **What type of trap seal loss can occur at the base of a discharge stack due to the positive pressure produced in the stack itself?**

○ a   Self-siphonage
○ b   Evaporation
○ c   Induced siphonage
◉ d   Compression.

Answer d
Positive pressure or compression can occur at the base of a stack due to restriction created by the bend at the foot of the stack. The other types of trap seal loss are not normally associated with problems at the base of the stack.

5   A branch connection should NOT be made into a discharge stack serving a two-storey property within what vertical dimension of the drain invert?

- ○ a   200 mm
- ○ b   350 mm
- ◉ c   450 mm
- ○ d   600 mm.

Answer c
The Building Regulations Approved Document H Section 1.11 dictates that a distance of 450 mm should be left between the invert of the drain and the lowest branch connection in a two-storey property; three to five storeys, the distance increases to 750 mm; over five storeys, all ground-floor appliances must have their own stack.

6   What is the minimum size of discharge stack that can be used in a two-storey property?

- ○ a   50 mm
- ◉ b   75 mm
- ○ c   100 mm
- ○ d   150 mm

Answer b
The Building Regulations Approved Document H Section 1.28 gives the smallest size for a soil stack with a WC with an outlet less than 80 mm as being served by a 75 mm diameter soil stack. Soil stacks with WCs with outlets above 80 mm should be served by a 100 mm minimum diameter stack. The soil stack should not be less than largest appliance trap connecting to it.

7   In the following diagram, the trap seal is shown at dimension

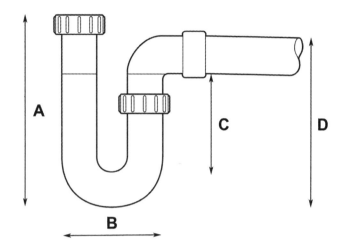

○ a   A
○ b   B
◉ c   C
○ d   D.

Answer c

The seal of a trap is the measurement from the top of the trap bend to the top of the weir point of the connection to the discharge pipework, this giving the depth of water that forms a seal as shown in dimension C.

8   Which one of the following is suitable for use when making a branch connection into a discharge stack immediately opposite another branch connection?

○ a   A strap boss with swept entry
◉ b   A junction with swept entry
○ c   A boss pipe with 90° entry
○ d   A junction with 90° entry.

Answer b

90° or oblique entry methods immediately opposite another branch connection into a discharge stack are not permissible and connections of this type must be staggered. The exception to the rule is when a swept entry connection is used.

Notes

9   Why should an air-admittance valve NOT be installed in a very dusty environment?

○ a   The rubber diaphragm will perish quickly
◉ b   The filter will be prone to continual blocking
○ c   The valve will suffer from excessive corrosion
○ d   The valve will rupture due to excessive pressure.

Answer b
Air-admittance valves require unobstructed access to the atmosphere to work correctly; dust can block the filter of an air-admittance valve and cause it to stop working, as it would not allow the admittance of air into the system.

10 What trap-seal depth must be used when connecting a kitchen sink directly to a below-ground drainage system?

○ a   19 mm
○ b   38 mm
○ c   50 mm
◉ d   75 mm.

Answer d
The Building Regulations Approved Document H Section 1.4 states that, regardless of where a kitchen sink is connected to the drainage system, a minimum trap seal of 75 mm is required.

Knowledge learning outcome 3
Know the site preparation techniques for sanitary appliances and connecting pipework systems

11 Which British Standard makes recommendations on the activity space that should be provided around sanitary appliances?

○ a   BS 5440
◉ b   BS 6465
○ c   BS EN 12056
○ d   BS EN 12983.

Answer b
BS 6465 (option b) gives recommendations on the design of sanitary facilities. It covers the recommended spacing requirements for sanitary appliances in order for them to be satisfactorily used by people.

Notes

12 What is the maximum depth of pipe notch that can be cut in a first-floor joist that has a depth of 250 mm?

- ○ a   22 mm
- ◉ b   31 mm
- ○ c   52 mm
- ○ d   67 mm.

Answer b

The maximum depth of notch for pipework passing through structural timbers is the depth of the joist divided by 8. So in this case the calculation would be 250 mm ÷ 8 = 31.25 mm, rounded to the nearest millimetre gives 31 mm.

13 The component in the following photograph is used for connecting

- ○ a   two PVC-u pipes together
- ◉ b   a PVC-u pipe to a clay drain
- ○ c   a PVC-u pipe to a WC pan
- ○ d   two PVC-u pipes to a bath.

Answer b

The fitting pictured is used to make a PVC-u pipework connection to a clay drainage pipe. A sand and cement mortar joint is then made between the clay pipe socket and the PVC-u fitting.

Notes

14 Which one of the following can be used for removing a blockage in a waste pipe?

- ⦿ a   An auger
- ◯ b   A gulley grab
- ◯ c   A drain plug
- ◯ d   A siphon.

Answer a

Drain augers are designed to clear blockages in waste and soil pipes close to the point of use. A drain auger can be manual or powered and it uses high grade, non-kink rust-resistant spring steel wire to burrow through blockages. The other options would not be used for clearing a blockage in a narrow-diameter waste pipe.

Knowledge learning outcome 4
Know the installation requirements of sanitary appliances and connecting pipework systems

15 The seal between a close-coupled WC flushing cistern and its pan is made watertight by using

- ◯ a   silicone sealant
- ◯ b   a 'top hat' washer
- ⦿ c   a 'doughnut' washer
- ◯ d   putty and paste.

Answer c

A 'doughnut' washer is a large washer made from rubber or dense foam to form the seal between the flush-pipe outlet of a close-coupled cistern and the WC pan; this is held in place by the retaining bolts of the cistern pulling the cistern and the pan together.

16 Why should a gap be left in a ring-seal joint (as shown in the diagram) between the pipe ends and fitting shoulders?

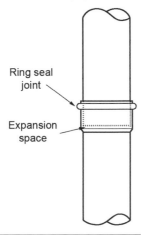

Ring seal joint

Expansion space

- ○ a   To protect against the risk of fire
- ◉ b   To permit thermal movement
- ○ c   To permit access for maintenance
- ○ d   To protect against trap-seal loss.

Answer b

The Building Regulations Approved Document H Section 1.35 states that all jointing that takes place should fully support the pipework and not restrict thermal movement; by leaving a small gap in ring seal joints it will allow thermal movement to take place without compromising the fitting.

17 By how much would 10 m of PVC-u pipe expand if it were to be heated from 10°C to 40°C and its coefficient of linear expansion was 0.06 mm/m/°C?

- ○ a   7 mm
- ○ b   12 mm
- ◉ c   18 mm
- ○ d   25 mm.

Answer c

The coefficient of linear expansion of PVC-u is 0.06 mm/m/°C. To complete this calculation we must find and fill in the numbers in the equation. The length of pipe is 10 m. The temperature difference is 40°C minus 10°C equals 30°C.

When we place them into the equation we get 0.06 mm x 10 x 30 = 18 mm.

18 Which one of the following is a suitable fixing for a wash hand basin?

○ a   Steel screw
◉ b   Brass screw
○ c   Copper nail
○ d   Steel bolt.

Answer b
Because of the environment of wash hand basins being damp or wet a large proportion of the time, the use of a fixing that would corrode would be unacceptable (options a and d). A brass (option b) or stainless steel screw would be the only method of fixing that would allow for continued support. A copper nail is unacceptable as the fixing must be easily removed.

19 A waste appliance can discharge into a

○ a   soakaway
○ b   surface water drain
◉ c   foul-water drain
○ d   water main.

Answer c
Waste appliances must be connected to the foul water drainage system; the other options would give rise to contamination of the surface water locally (option a) or regionally (option b). Option d is not associated with a sanitation system.

20 A branchpipe discharging to a new gulley should terminate

○ a   above the gulley grid
◉ b   below the gulley grid
○ c   below the gulley water seal
○ d   through the gulley water seal.

Answer b
The Building Regulations Approved Document H Section 1.13 states that any branch pipe discharging to a gully should terminate between the grating or sealing plate and the top of the water seal, as detailed in option b.

21 When jointing a new waste strap boss to an existing painted PVC-u discharge stack, which one of the following should form part of the jointing process?

◉ a   Removal of the paint in the proposed strap boss location
○ b   Repainting of the stack in the proposed strap boss location
○ c   Use of white spirit to make the joint between boss and stack
○ d   Use of linseed oil putty to make the joint between boss and stack.

Answer a
When preparing an area for connection of a strap boss it is important that all dust dirt, paint (option a) and debris be removed from the connection location to allow the sealant used to make the joint between the boss and the soil stack watertight.

Knowledge learning outcome 5
Know the service and maintenance requirements of sanitary appliances and connecting pipework systems

22 Which one of the following is the most likely cause of a drop valve constantly discharging water into a WC pan?

○ a   Siphon washer failure
○ b   Service valve failure
◉ c   Grit on the drop valve seal
○ d   Blockage of the overflow.

Answer c
A siphon washer (option a) is not fitted in a drop valve. Neither an overflow blockage (option d) or a service valve failure (option b) would cause a drop valve to constantly discharge water. Grit on the valve seal would however potentially cause a drop valve to constantly discharge water (option c) and is a commonly occurring fault.

Notes

23 A blockage in a waste appliance trap can be removed by using

○ a   drain rods
◉ b   a force cup
○ c   a gulley grab
○ d   silicone sealant.

Answer b
A force cup is a term for a type of plunger. The device is commonly used to create pressure and unblock waste traps.

24 Which one of the following is most likely to be included on a record completed during the scheduled maintenance of a sanitation system?

○ a   A check to confirm that all traps have been replaced
○ b   The replacement of 'o' ring seals on all pipework joints
○ c   The application of new glue to all solvent welded joints
◉ d   A check to confirm that pipework is correctly supported.

Answer d
Of the options listed, a check for correct pipework support (option d) is the only item that would be performed during a periodic maintenance inspection.

Knowledge learning outcome 6
Know the decommissioning requirements of sanitary appliances and connecting pipework systems

25 When taking sanitary appliances out of use in order to work on them, isolation of which one of the following will cause the greatest disruption to the occupants of dwellings?

○ a   Sinks
○ b   Baths
○ c   Wash hand basins.
◉ d   WCs

Answer d

The WC is the most fundamental of all the sanitary appliances listed, as washing (option b), preparing food (option a) or hand washing (option c) can be delayed or alternative arrangements can be made, but toilets cannot easily be replaced temporarily.

26 **When removing a WC pan connected to an existing sanitary pipework system, which one of the following is considered to be the main nuisance if the pan is to be left disconnected for a significant period of time?**

- ○ a   Noise
- ◉ b   Smells
- ○ c   Dust production
- ○ d   Fire risk.

Answer b

The removal of the WC pan will break the seal of the sanitation system and allow noxious fumes from the drains to enter the premises.

27 **Which one of the following will fully prevent a WC from being flushed while work is taking place on a sanitary pipework system?**

- ◉ a   Isolation of the water supply and emptying of the cistern
- ○ b   Temporary capping of the sanitary pipework with a drain plug
- ○ c   Covering the top of the WC pan with cling film
- ○ d   Use of a warning notice placed on the WC pan.

Answer a

Option b would prevent the WC from discharging to the sewer, but not stop its operation. Option d would advise that a WC should not be used but again would not prevent use. Option c would not prevent flushing at all. The only method that would prevent the operation of the WC would be to remove the WC's cistern ability to flush, such as identified in option a.

Knowledge learning outcome 7
Know the inspection and soundness testing requirements
of sanitary appliances and connecting pipework systems

28 Which one of the following would be included in a visual
inspection of a new sanitary appliance system as part of
the commissioning process?

- ● a   Check for overall compliance of the installation with
statutory regulations
- ○ b   Check for operation to ensure that trap seals are not lost
during operation
- ○ c   Confirmation that all branch pipework includes a ventilating pipe
- ○ d   Confirmation that the system will be disinfected as part of
commissioning.

Answer a
A visual inspection carried out before the system is charged and tested
will include the following:
- All correct pipework joints have been made – no open ends etc
- All pipework fixings are properly made and adequate provision for
thermal expansion has been made
- The installation of the system (and components) is compliant with
the requirements of Building Regulations Part H.

29 During a pressure test on a sanitary pipework system,
the pressure in the system is raised using

- ○ a   a hydraulic test kit
- ● b   hand bellows
- ○ c   a manometer
- ○ d   a foot pump.

Answer b
Soundness testing of sanitary pipework is carried out with air; the test kit
for sanitary pipework contains:
- Manometer
- Hand bellows
- Hose
- Y piece
- Hollow plugs and/or inflatable stopper(s) – if required

It is the hand bellows that are used to raise the system pressure.

30 A leak can be detected on a plastic sanitary pipework system during pressure testing by

Notes

- ⊙ a   using soap solution
- ○ b   using a gas detector
- ○ c   wrapping joints with paper
- ○ d   looking for signs of smoke.

Answer a

The Building Regulations Approved Document H Section 1.38 states that smoke testing is not recommended for PVC-u pipework soundness testing (option d). A gas detector would not detect leaks (option b). As the test is carried out with air, option c would not be effective. Taking this into account, the best option for locating leaks would be soap solution (option a).

Notes

Answer key

Sample test 6189-010

Question	Answer	Question	Answer
1	c	16	b
2	b	17	c
3	a	18	b
4	d	19	c
5	c	20	b
6	b	21	a
7	c	22	c
8	b	23	b
9	b	24	d
10	d	25	d
11	b	26	b
12	b	27	a
13	b	28	a
14	a	29	b
15	c	30	a

More information

More information

Notes

Further reading

Required reading
Maskrey, Michael B., *The City & Guilds Textbook: NVQ Level 2 Diploma in Plumbing & Heating*
Publication date: Spring/Summer 2010

Additional reading
HSE publications and guidance notes – Numerous publications on all aspects of health and safety and methods of complying with health and safety law. Details of HSE free and costed publications can be accessed at www.hse.gov.uk.

Energy Savings Trust publications and guidance notes – Numerous publications and guidance notes on the energy-efficient installation of fossil fuel-burning heating appliances and environmental technologies. Documents can be freely accessed at www.est.org.uk.

Building Regulations Approved Documents (Technical Booklets in Northern Ireland) – Series of technical documents identifying methods of installing plumbing and heating systems in compliance with the Building Regulations (may be freely downloaded from www.planningportal.gov.uk in England and Wales or www.dfpni.gov.uk in Northern Ireland).
– A – Structure (D in NI)
– G – Sanitation, hot water safety and water efficiency (P in NI)
– H – Drainage and waste disposal (N in NI)
– L1 – Conservation of fuel and power (F1 in NI)

Domestic Building Services Compliance Guide – A technical document outlining the energy-efficient standards of heating and hot water system installation (may be freely downloaded from www.planningportal.gov.uk).

Defra Guidance to the Water Regulations – A guide to the technical requirements of installing plumbing and heating systems in compliance with the Water Regulations (freely accessible at www.defra.gov.uk).

Laurie Young & Graham Mays, *Water Regulations Guide*, published by WRAS, 2000

CIBSE, *Domestic Heating Design Guide*, published by CIBSE, 2007

Relevant British Standard publications
- BS 6465: 2 – Code of practice for space requirements
  for sanitary appliances
- BS 6700 – Design, installation, testing and maintenance
  of services supplying water for domestic use within buildings
  and their curtilages
- BS 8000: 13 – Workmanship on building sites. Code of practice
  for above-ground drainage and sanitary appliances
- BS 8000: 15 – Workmanship on building sites. Code of practice
  for hot and cold water services (domestic scale)
- BS EN 12056: 2 – Gravity drainage systems inside buildings.
  Sanitary pipework, layout and calculation
- BS EN 12056: 3 – Gravity drainage systems inside buildings.
  Roof drainage, layout and calculation

Notes

Notes

Online resources

City & Guilds www.cityandguilds.com
The City & Guilds website can give you more information about studying for
further professional and vocational qualifications to advance your personal
or career development, as well as locations of centres that provide courses.

SmartScreen www.smartscreen.co.uk
City & Guilds' dedicated online support portal SmartScreen provides learner
and tutor support for over 100 City & Guilds qualifications. It helps engage
learners in the excitement of learning and enables tutors to free up more
time to do what they love most – teach!

APHC www.aphc.co.uk
The trade association for plumbing and heating contractors.

British Standards Institution www.bsi-group.com
Produces national and international standards documents.

CIPHE www.ciphe.org.uk
The professional institute for the plumbing and heating industry.

CLG www.communities.gov.uk
Government department responsible for Building Regulations.

DEFRA www.defra.gov.uk
Government department responsible for Water Regulations.

Energy Savings Trust www.est.org.uk
The UK's leading impartial organisation which helps people to save
energy and reduce carbon emissions.

HSE www.hse.gov.uk
HSE is the national independent watchdog for work-related health,
safety and illness.

HVCA www.hvca.org.uk
The trade association for heating and ventilation contractors.

JIB for PMES www.jib-pmes.org.uk

Sets terms and conditions for plumbing operatives and provides the registration body function for the plumbing industry in England and Wales.

Planning Portal www.planningportal.gov.uk

The UK Government's online planning and building regulations resource.

SummitSkills www.summitskills.org.uk

The sector Skills Council for the building services engineering sector, dealing with skills development and education matters in the sector.

UK Copper Board www.ukcopperboard.co.uk

Promotes the benefits of copper plumbing and heating systems to the construction industry.

Water Regulations Advisory Scheme www.wras.co.uk

Leading authority on Water Regulations in the UK.

Notes

Notes

Further courses

City & Guilds NVQ Level 3 Diploma in Plumbing & Heating or Domestic Heating (6189)

A natural progression from the City & Guilds NVQ Level 2 Diploma in Plumbing & Heating or Domestic Heating (6189). These qualifications allow learners to become competent to industry standards in plumbing and domestic heating at a supervisory level. Four pathways are available through the Level 3 qualifications including gas, oil, solid fuel and environmental technologies. Anyone wishing to become recognised as a domestic plumber or heating engineer, including running a business, should consider these qualifications.

City & Guilds NVQ Diploma in Heating & Ventilating (6188)

These qualifications provide learners with the skills to install, commission or maintain, and have knowledge of industrial and commercial heating and ventilation systems. The outcomes are in line with industry standards.

City & Guilds NVQ Diploma in Refrigeration and Air Conditioning (6187)

Taking these qualifications gives learners the skills to install, commission or maintain refrigeration and air conditioning systems to industry standards.

City & Guilds Domestic Gas Installation and Maintenance (6014)

This qualification is aimed at learners who wish to pursue a specialist heating career in gas installation, service and maintenance. It is also suitable for candidates who are undertaking apprenticeships. The main aim is to qualify people to work in domestic properties and households on gas appliances and systems. This qualification is also appropriate for existing experienced gas fitters who want to be assessed against current gas national standards and gain an up-to-date gas qualification.

City & Guilds NVQ Level 4 Higher Professional Diploma in Building Services Engineering (4467)

Designed for high-achieving individuals developing a career in the building services industry. It provides a broad understanding of the variety of high-level roles available and the skills needed for them.

City & Guilds Award in F-Gas and ODS Regulations (2079)

This qualification provides existing skilled workers with the skills and knowledge to handle F-gas ODS safely, in line with legislation.

City & Guilds Award in Environmental Technologies (2399)
This qualification provides existing skilled workers with the skills and knowledge required to install and maintain environmental technology systems, including solar photovoltaic, solar thermal, heat pumps and water recycling. An additional Level 2 qualification provides learners with an overview of these emerging technologies, allowing them to provide initial advice and guidance.

Notes

Notes